Selected Poems 1971-2017

Also by Laurie Duggan

Poetry

East: Poems 1970–74 (1976)
Under the Weather (1978)
East and Under the Weather (2014)
Adventures in Paradise (1982, 1991)
The Great Divide, Poems 1973–83 (1985)
The Ash Range (1987; 2nd edition, 2005*)
The Epigrams of Martial (1989, 2010)
Blue Notes (1990)
The Home Paddock (1991)
Memorials (1996)
New and Selected Poems, 1971–1993 (1996)
Mangroves (2003)
Compared to What: Selected Poems 1971–2003 (2005) *
The Passenger (2006)
Crab & Winkle (2009) *
The Collected Blue Hills (2011)
The Pursuit of Happiness (2012) *
Allotments (2014) *
No particular place to go (2017) *

Cultural history

Ghost Nation (2001)

* *Shearsman titles*

Laurie Duggan

Selected Poems
1971-2017

Shearsman Books

First published in the United Kingdom in 2018 by
Shearsman Books
50 Westons Hill Drive
Emersons Green
BRISTOL
BS16 7DF

www.shearsman.com

ISBN 978-1-84861-573-1

ACKNOWLEDGEMENTS

I would like to thank all of the presses large and small that have produced my
work over the years: Rigmarole of the Hours (Melbourne), Wild & Woolley
(Sydney), the Experimental Art Foundation (Adelaide), Hale & Iremonger
(Sydney), Picador (Australia), Northern Lights (London), Nicholas Pounder
(Sydney), Scripsi (Melbourne), Little Esther (Adelaide), Noone's Press
(Melbourne), University of Queensland Press (Brisbane), Vagabond (Sydney),
Pressed Wafer (Boston), Fewer & Further (Wendell, MA), Donnithorne Street
Press (Kyneton, Vic), Light-Trap Press (Brisbane), Puncher & Wattman
(Sydney), and of course Shearsman Books (Exeter and Bristol).
Additionally several poems not previously published in book form have
appeared in: *Broadsheet* (NZ), *Overland* (Melbourne) and in Corey Wakeling
& Jeremy Balius (eds), *Outcrop: radical Australian poetry of land*,
Fremantle, WA: Black Rider Press, 2013.

There are numerous people who deserve thanks for what's contained here.
In particular I'd like to thank John Scott, Alan Wearne, Pam Brown, Ken
Bolton, Gig Ryan, August Kleinzahler, Basil and Martha King, Tony Baker,
Martin Duwell, Angela Gardner, Ian Brinton and Paul Rossiter. John Forbes,
Peter Porter, Gael Turnbull, Ed Dorn, Roy Fisher, Jonathan Williams and Lee
Harwood are no longer with us but each one of them was generous with help
and encouragement at the right moments. There are so many others who have
helped out with all kinds of things. Hopefully you know who you are!

Finally I would like to thank Rosemary Hunter without whom
so much of this would not have been possible.

Contents

Four / 1986–1994

Five / 2000–2006

One

1971-1984

Cockatoo Draft

for John & Lyn Hughes

How can I comprehend
                              Christmas morning
                    cloud across the Dandenong Ranges
                    sponge squeezed over the tilled field
                              the back hills under mist
                                        foliage dense, clotted,
                    a treeline like brushed ink,
                              lit shafts of trunk stripped of bark.

Hack down berries round the fig tree,
shovel scraps, old toy vehicles, bottles
                    lean on an N-frame gate in a swarm of flies
                    (a tractor, distant in the gully)
                    long black-tailed birds pick strawberries
                              whole rows rot.

                              Night frogs in the dam
                              the galaxies explode
                    in a room painted black
                    I read Adamson's Rumour

difficult, without a survey map
          to see where I will be taken,
adapting Wordsworth or Snyder to see those blue ranges toward Warbur-
ton.

                                        *

Areas of ploughed, cleared,
                    & wooded land,
                    thick bush of the state forest,
          walking up Mountain Rd. curve   a lone tree
                    dipped in the landscape.

Sit on a pine trunk at the road's junction,
a dam in the cleft southward
chrome yellow flowers on a slope due east;
Cockatoo, a clearing on the opposite hillside

A spiderweb shines from its frame of thistles
the 'sole arabian tree' bursts from confinement
watch the hills
move into their stillness
work against the light
pick on the downward slope
wild strawberries
between the rows.

Post-War

Lights burn in houses we are not, through
fear or ignorance, permitted to enter;
the hotel we visit in darkness
remains nameless   streaming from the balcony
expensive underwear of *übermenschen*,
clown masks, balloons, whistles.
A blind accordionist floats across the suburbs
as if, from the brick and bone-dust, something
more than tangible can emerge.
In Berlin the balloons drift upward
on the pitch of a tide, as biplanes
descended on Lens.
Lost for images, we become the fleeing crowd:
a mouth swallowed the whole picture.

Years after the promise receded,
through the hard winter, men wander
aimlessly by the tracks, boxcars
branded by number,
convicted,
sentenced:
Scott's Run, West Virginia, 1937.
Figures in a caravan, huddled in pale incandescence
as whores who spurn commerce
summon a trite poetic.
The movement is into form;
the flux contained, the moment passes:
subject, object, fall into place as
starched gestures of shirts over the hotel.

Bridge Road

save the language from poetic tongue

'milk bar' is accessible but
'tangible' is not

Hello Lenin!

help, I'm trapped in this
chip packet

right you are, son

he wiped his moustache

the cat nuzzled the chips box

it was 11.40 p.m.

*

'Could you work in
a place like that?'

(a paper factory)

outside it looked
& felt like rain

'it always does
in Alexandria'

*

In a strange way
I like this place.
Cook spaghetti Bolognese

Eat it to 'Books and Ideas'
spit and swear at
Roland Robinson

Tom, you shit
(the cat) . . . out
of the sink!

from A Skater on the Sara River

Dec. 27th

> white mist in the gullies near Jerusalem Inlet
> the radio fades,   cuts out
> Bob Evans passes a plastic bag
> chicken & ham pieces

       *

> Singleton lights up ahead

> we wake up
>   with the first joint.

       *

> trace marks in sand
>   bright weeds
>   the morning red
>   under rain
> the 'Guy Fawkes' or 'Little River'
> down on the flood season
>   insects float above the Sara
>   light up in the air
>   orange on the far bank,
> the directional sense of a caterpillar
>   on a trunk, shadow side
>   from the rain
> everything specific.

> a skater on the Sara River
> hovers on a flat of granite

from North

for Lesley Gilette

        sleet over the orchard
            cut loganberries
        dry later in the sun

& rain on the roof.
            the Post Office
minus furniture.   walls painted ivory.
through the window Terry & Steve
chop a truckload of wood.
              At night
wind comes from the west.

        Armidale
        airfield blown flat
        pink blossoms.

        driver of taxi reckons a tyre
of the Euclid setup worth more than
his whole outfit.

        *

        mountain

& rocks

                  ridge
            a
        on
      town
    a

North   South

        so.

sunrise & sunset painted
on E & W shopfronts

      the light over a
      verandah
      descending into
      hotel rooms

   bed on the floor; the iron sagging

& the doors left open
   faced with hillsides towards
     Tuntable Falls

    *

    north: the peak of Mt Warning
   volcanic plug like the toe of a giant
or (Lesley): peaked & bent hat of
a witch. directions difficult
in the almost complete circle of
mts round Murwillumbah. even the sun
seems to confuse here.

  a train cutting
through the landscape to the north
sounds out over the valley.
   dust of stars on the porch,
Stoker's Siding

  in the pub, between sets
Dave Kelly plays Ray Charles
the band at beer

from More North

for Terry Larsen & Lorraine Osborn

10/1/76

     a stormy sky like Elsheimer's
     – moon riding on a bank of cloud
     Movement across from (Jess:)
            'the dirty corner' (E. - S.E.)

     & the next morning
           heavy rain
                 from the cot
                 in the old post-office
     early daylight
                 thunder
     Lorraine & Bob still asleep

     (Jess on the party slowly breaking up:)
     'It's like having teeth out
     one at a time'

from Spleen

my birthday
a hangover
& the drums upstairs!

on the ferry
        Ry Cooder's 'Dark End of the Street'

outside Luna Park
        'hello pussy cat'

I eat a birthday dinner
in the Malaya restaurant

4,000 CAR DEALERS QUIT

A note

Huntingdale & Metropolitan golf links / bunker fuck mythology

            Doveton High's
            amazing pregnancy ratio

         and the naked Mr Clayton who
         rode buggy to the beach over swampland
            – this all we got of local lore
      to present/know that much of an area
      as Alan Wearne, his poems,
            their real history

Windsor Rd
& the legendary Forbes –
      golf-links perve
      nobody ever saw

                Simon Stevens
                – Sex Pistol before his time

Down the Coast

for Denis Gallagher

    Dapto

           a bathtub in a paddock

    Berry

           a hand comes out of the hillside
                holding a milk bottle

Lonnie Mack   Rolling Stones   Elvin Bishop

       *

days before the huge fireplace
Dennis & Kerry's

          out, the hill slope &
             bare plum tree

      Japonoiserie

          sky clears to the south

through the kitchen window
          in three panels
the long down slope   a treeless hill section
two car roofs, then, in the last frame
          the plum tree branches

Kikkoman   Tequila   National Panasonic

          things slow down

       *

Metta: 'We've got to run fast
          It stops the rain from
             getting us wet.'

the dog & cat are both
'Tiny Tina Thatcher'

        through the bathroom window
           a distant cow

    *

      wake up in front of the fireplace
      after a strange dream
      china blue walls
      the white board ceiling
      cross rail of an old classroom

      on the mantelpiece
          Kwannon
      a sense of order

    *

Anna & Ken's blue V.W. crawls up the opposite hill
off for milk   cottage pie ingredients

tiny birds in the plum

      fine   high striated clouds

Garfield circled by hills
timber trucks emerge briefly then disappear

      clear morning   Claremont
      a strong wind blows in towards Bemboka
      rustles dead leaves of the choko
      bells rattle on corrugated tin

      two poplars
      acid green paddocks

    *

on the living room piano
12 bar blues

      Anna bicycles across Johnson Ck. bridge

in the middle of a field
a horse turns to listen

           wind veers round to N.W.

& on the piano

           'For No One'

       *

long night drive over timber tracks
          & stony creek beds
             to a restaurant?

     Cuttagee Lake   lightning miles out
     the milky way overhead

         & after every wave
         tiny luminous creatures on the sand

Newman Street

orange & white pots
square in the middle of the sill
        of the house opposite
its blind always half-drawn over curtains

a mirror image to this house
the rooms must be the same shape

a large woman leans over the fence
appearing impassive

the sun moves across her face

*

across on the corner of the street
a house yard surrounded by a cyclone fence
young couples often stand examining
        pieces of wrought iron

*

the TV set doesn't work properly
it's lost its vertical hold
actors feet hang from the top of the screen
        over their talking heads

*

the corner milk bar is often out of milk
the red phone isn't always there

Peasant Mandarin

The pasture's dry
and the mare's near foaling;
no worries! Our Les
keeps the subsidy rolling.

The Bunyah lad's wrinkled,
confessed, come clean,
whose baby eyes twinkled
like an M-16;

the early target practice,
the quick translations
from Weatherboard Cathedral
to United Nations

furthered through
editorship and prayer
falling from lips
in the Chatswood air:

God bless Doug Anthony,
the Pope, St Peter,
the Liberal Party,
the illusion of metre

in English verse written
as she is spoke
by the absolutely
ordinary bloke.

To all things a season,
to harvest, to plant,
to jet Midwest
on a Guggenheim grant,

to shun international
modernist glam
in Merthyr Tydfil
and Amsterdam.

Nothing really changes:
the Holy Ghost
supports dairy farmers
on the central coast,

Thomas W. Shapcott's
the new Mackaness,
Red Movie's author's
the new red menace.......

The pastures dry up
and the crows get the sheep;
in the suburbs, a poet
turns in his sleep.

They can't take that away from me

for Morgan Smith

A truck with an enormous panda
passes the library window.

lunch time.

         *

spiderweb tattoo on an elbow
       protruding from a Bedford van
           12.00 p.m. 22/4/1980
(Hasn't worked for months?)

         *

Coogee smog fades out
          Over the Pacific
it's silent off the main street.

         *

A painting by a Korean child
showing five (obviously Korean)
children near a conifer. Two
dance together, two are running
and one, by himself, is looking
up the near-conical trunk of the
tree which seems in its height
to leave the perspective of the
painting behind.

A cracked green (glazed) ashtray,
always full.

Several late 1950s and early 1960s issues of Argosy and Meanjin magazines at the top of a stepped bookcase.

A red and white checked curtain.

A blue corduroy dressing gown and a black silk dressing gown both without fasteners and split along the seams.

A reproduction of 'Café at Night', September 1888, by Vincent Van Gogh.

A reproduction of a painting by a naïve artist showing four old women around a table playing dominoes. The sharpness of the outline and the silhouetted black stove and table legs make it look like the work of one of the Nabis.

A black and white photograph taken at Writers' Week of the 1964 Adelaide Festival. Douglas Stewart, David Rowbotham, Kenneth Slessor, and Kym Bonython are clearly identifiable.

A long red-edged desk with a built-in paper shelf underneath it.

An old desk typewriter, a small portable, and a large newer portable typewriter.

A white dressing table with a
pile of assorted shoes underneath
it.

An art deco bedside lamp with a
square wooden base and a
hemispherical dented metal shade
which rotates to direct the light
of a weak bulb.

A wood floor with a patterned
grass mat, light, with purple
bands across it.

A square white clock with a
blue face.

*

Anzac day
silence out of
which nothing comes. Grey cat on vermilion floor.
Coffee pot, milk carton, sugar bowl & mugs. Radiator. Iron. Table of books
& junk. Roll of pink paper. Sock on elastic length. TV with bent leg.
Green wooden umbrella. Brown polyester socks. Wool pieces. Boxes of records.
Wires. Dictionary. Liquorice.

Yellow raincoat over a rope.

Broken typewriter.

Green toy soldiers in a plastic bag look like a
deal of dope.

EXPRESSIONISM

Echo Beach

*

Everything passes into history
The axe falls & the trunk splits
steam floats away from the tea cup
Only shape affects us unpredictably
      – there's nothing nostalgic
            about cartography –
(some get sentimental about
      roads obliterated by wings
          of new buildings
but block lettered names of suburbs
      become wholly abstract – as much
      part of the pattern as drainage channels

          *

(Song: 'They Can't Take That
            Away From Me')

      – it was in some musical? –

          I got a whole emotional vocabulary
          out of the movies

          *

Lying in the sun on Morgan's bed
while she's out visiting a friend
of her mother's.
             Just packed
a bag of my things from her wardrobe
& books from the floor. I lie down to read
poems by Charles Reznikoff.

      (In the letterbox
      a copy of
        PERV
      magazine)

                              Finish the last
           clues of *Sydney Morning Herald*
           Cryptic Crossword No. 9666.

                              *

                 pale blue enamel white flower doorknob
           Japanese print behind glass, leaning on the desk

           Yellow bowl with blue hand-painted decoration
           London Palladium program next to British Railways'
                 1950s watercolour of a fast train
                 crossing a viaduct

                              *

<u>College lawn notes</u>   An awareness of mutability. Nothing lasts. The
most terrifying of the concentration camp photos are the ones of the
piles of cases, glasses &c. The Life Studies, Plath, Berryman writers sen-
timentally over-value their humanism – what they write is like knitting a
jumper to wear in heaven. Human beings aren't finally all that important.
I'd sooner be an archaeologist concerned with the teaspooons and pot
hangers of an age

                              *

                 Vienna Coffee   70c
                 Cinnamon Toast   80c

           The *Blue & Gold* Restaurant
                 George St.

                              *

I would like to write poems like Edward Hopper paintings. The quality
of light through the glass, the shape of the coffee machine & the reflec-
tion of the electrical sign – all absolutely right.

                              *

Trying to look hard at something, my eyes glaze over – the *idea* of appearances takes over from observation (which works more in the way a sneak photographer would – you don't really see the photographs until they're developed – and the scene is no longer before you).

*

Is this making of statements on poetics with no audience some kind of madness?

*

Order is entirely the work of the imagination. Everything else is data-blizzard. [People like to talk about ethics but everyone is basically a soul-murderer. To claim holiness is to deny it to other beings. (All religions are basically imperialistic).]

*

Square brackets indicate craziness!
(What do I think I am . . . a thinker!?!)

*

I've never *wanted* to write poems

*

dangers – the MAUDLIN

sentimental attachment to *things*
as *representative* of people.

I wrote poems by default
(because there was no other nominal area
that would accommodate what I was doing.)

What I want to do is write
s/t really *strong*

man covers his nose
[&] hunches forward
up Bathurst St.

*

Impaludism (O.E.D.) 1881
– The general morbid state occurring in
inhabitants of marshy districts.

(sounds like modern English poetry)

*

Elocution Exercise: Small Portuguese are more pleasing than
                             awkward Australians.

*

Ted Berrigan reminds John Forbes of me – especially the bit about the
toilet paper.

*

I don't even like found poems much anymore because too
many of them sound too much like poetry to begin with.

*

VEHICLES OBSTRUCTING ACCESS WILL BE TOWED AWAY.

Adventures in Paradise

for John Forbes, John Scott, & Carl Harrison-Ford

Near the end of the thirty-first year of my life
I find myself a bundle of sweaty neurones
under an umbrella shade in the courtyard
of the old Sydney University Union building.
What do I reckon has got me here and how?
I make a start on this autobiography.

Firstly, being a baby in baby powder
listening to Haydn and being fed
by an implement I think was called a pusher.
My grandmother wouldn't let my mother
hold me up in the bath. Is this
psychology? I don't remember much else.

Photographs give a few important clues:
the pattern of my father's cardigan
when he stood holding me up on the gate
at Beaconsfield Parade, South Melbourne.
I must have been looking out straight
across the road to Port Phillip Bay.

Then I'm sitting in a fruit box in the yard
with a dog called Sandy whose bones
I used to share. The place was a guest house
owned by my grandmother. I talked before
I could walk. Crawled up the stairs.
A man called Len Lovell fell off the roof.

The famous jazz musician Johnny Sangster
was a bohemian who lived in a bungalow
out the back. Upstairs there was a gangster
– incognito – who later got shot on the pier
in broad daylight. His real name was Freddy
Harrison. He held me at the breakfast table.

A lady threw lollies into the yard from the flat
next door. In a photograph we had cracked lino
on the dining room table and floor
and a Metters Early Kooka. My grandmother
had the room with the balcony upstairs.
Mussel and seaweed smells came from the shore.

My parents moved to Clayton when I was four
(this sounds like a line out of twelve-bar blues).
Every few months a man would come in a truck
and give me a few shillings for the empty
booze bottles which Dad stacked behind the garage.
Grandpa got caught on the dunny by the dunnyman.

When we got there the street was all mud
deep enough to swallow a baby, too deep
for cars. But we didn't have a car anyway
until Dad bought a 1957 Holden, but then
they'd almost made the road and all the market
gardens had all gone and I was at school.

There was a bakery near the station and one day
when Dad was sheltering from the rain
on the way back from work, a kid inside
called him a sour faced old bastard.
It got pulled down, became a wedding
reception room, then a hairdressing salon.

The doctor lived on the main street until
he moved around the corner. He thought I was smart.
My grandmother didn't like Picasso – for her
the sole representative of 'Modern Art'. I wanted
to be a veterinary surgeon and fix up animals
and live on a farm like my uncle and aunt.

I went to Clayton South Primary School;
half the yard was covered in pine trees,
the other half was open for football and cricket.
The bodgies used to build houses out of

pine needles and go down there to smoke.
The milk got rancid in the morning sun.

On holidays I went with Mum and Dad
to Bairnsdale on the 'Gippslander' and caught
a bus up the Omeo highway. My uncle
and cousin drove up the back paddocks
in a 1928 Chev to fix the fences. Sometimes
we camped in a tent on the river bank.

A friend of my father's I used to call Uncle Pat
lived around Footscray and worked in the abattoirs.
He was thin from being in a concentration
camp. I caught a tram to the meatworks
and a man cut out a sheep's eye and stuck it
on a post. 'That's to see you don't get in trouble, Son.'

Another uncle worked in a recording studio
and my aunt had a program on the radio.
They got me to say a few things 'over the air'
and gave me a free ticket to the Tarax Happy Show.
I was in a play in kindergarten in a chorus
of policemen and solo as a kangaroo.

Mum read me Shakespeare's sonnets and Milton
before I could talk. I liked them
but I didn't like the poetry much at school.
I had to learn off something by John Masefield
about the sea that he wanted to sail a ship on,
heavily stressed. I thought all poets old and bald.

My fifth grade teacher thought the two best books
were the Bible and the Pilgrim's Progress
but I was more interested in the dinosaur
and fighter aircraft of the second world war.
I had a great uncle who copied out passages
from Tennyson on greeting cards in tiny writing.

Apart from that I didn't do very much.
I learned to ride a bike and went to high school

and got 27 for arithmetic in the second form.
I think I still wanted to be a Vet., though
cartography came next. I was in the Boy Scouts
and got wet sleeping under a picnic table.

I burst a blood vessel below the brain
and spent two months in the Alfred Hospital
reading the complete works of Ian Fleming
which I liked because he could make golf
interesting. Then I read Emile Zola
and started writing D.H. Lawrence imitations

in which young men full of spirit flung
themselves down on the earth and felt it breathe
and everything seemed complete. I wanted
to be a rock star, then a painter,
then a novelist, but I ended up writing poems
late in 1966, misunderstanding T.S. Eliot.

Next year I got into trouble for a satire
about Dame Zara Holt in the school magazine
that came out the week the Prime Minister
swam out to sea with his snorkel and wasn't seen
again. Australia was all the way with L.B.J.
and the girl I loved loved someone in the Labor Club.

I raged at Monash in check pants and a black
roll neck jumper. This was the age of 'progressive
rock'. Someone got into trouble for staging
a mock crucifixion outside the Union Caf.
The vice-chancellor sputtered about the disinterested
pursuit of knowledge. I stopped copying Keats

and started to copy William Carlos Williams:
the absurd sonnet turned into the stick poem.
Lots of grown up poets visited the university
and read to the Lit. Club, all pissed on flagon sherry.
Chris Wallace-Crabbe competed with billiards
near the billiard room and the billiards won.

Some of the other poetry was more fun,
like Robert King dancing to bongo drums
and ripping his shirt off, or when B.A. Breen
read concrete poems with repeated words and when
an old academic asked him his definition of verse
Rob Smyth chanted POETRY POETRY POETRY.

There were marbles under police horses' hooves
on the fourth of July, and Colin and Margaret
stared at candle flames while Iron Butterfly
played 'In-a-gadda-da-vida' and the doors
of perception opened wide. A weight ounce cost
twenty dollars. The 'underground' lived in Carlton.

Sometimes we'd drive in with boots of lager
to La Mama to hear some situationist verse.
I wrote a Dransfield parody: Acid Fuck Raga,
and got told off by Geoff Egglestone
for not taking *his* work seriously. It was bad
but the Melbourne Uni. poets were worse,

writing about martyrdom in Parkville
on mornings before lectures with the shakes;
imagining themselves as William Blakes.
Not long after this the combination of dope
and footnotes in the work of Alexander Pope
convinced me the era of the Stooge Effect had begun.

It was the dawning of the age of Aquarius.
I visited Sydney and wanted to stay there;
went to the Canberra Arts Festival with
a headband, two scarves, long hair, three sets
of beads and an army jacket and read to an audience
for the first time without going blind with fear.

Next year I moved to Sydney and a room
upstairs in Crown St., Surry Hills
with Pam Brown, poet, and an American groupie
with a waterbed and the bass player

from Led Zeppelin. Albie Thoms was shooting
funny movies about light from the front window.

Labor came into power. I missed the ballot box
and took a trip on a piece of blotting paper
thinking the party lights on trees in a Petersham park
had something to do with the advent of Socialism.
The blue V.W. spluttered through Glebe
bringing the pages of Zap Comix to life:

The me decade had begun. The age of subsidies,
safari suits, sonnet sequences, and the death of art.
The houses in the Glebe estate got repainted,
rents went up, people were psychoanalysed,
but all this seemed to happen very slowly.
I had a job in a public library

stamping out books, taking too many sick
days, moving out of too many houses
to return as a tourist and watch them stripped to brick.
Poetry too was beginning to wear its tweed
jacket again, and speak in muted tones
about the spiritually edifying architecture of Florence.

Briefly – I fell in and out of love
and in and out and in and out some more,
swore off drugs and took them up again,
finished two books and started on a third:
was granted a modest place on the honours list
whenever two other Sydney poets got together, pissed.

Blue Hills 2

Charles Demuth picture window
Room 2 – THE GRAND HOTEL – Bega
sunglasses perched on Frank Sinatra hat

    SUNSHINE
    on the side of a shed
    near the primary school
    washed out blue

Junction of the Brogo & Bega rivers,
one dry, one running under sand;
smoke haze as thick as Sydney smog

    – dried bamboo would explode
    if a match were lit

A crazed accountant sits at a desk in the park
On the desk
    Erica 4 Brian
    I WANT TO SUCK COCKS

    Log trucks cross the Bega flood bridge;
    all the poets have moved to Sydney

Blue Hills 4

clear prospective flotsam
from the bank of a near-dry creek;

axe sounds from the fire trail
& up there, a family

chain saw through black wattle &
red gum blocking the track.

mid-afternoon up at the house
the kitchen light dims,

porch chimes rattle, honeyeaters
flutter in the orchard:

return to the creek for a bath
& bring back the goat

as the rain shifts in from Bemboka

Blue Hills 11

a big pile of junk
bits of white plaster & blue fibre-board
rusted corrugated tin & broken bricks
marks on paper

> production of the
> ultimate artefact
> Ming vase
> über
> memorial ashtray

A prospect labelled:

> 'View of the Tasman Sea
> From Coalcliff Beach,
> Sunday 26th October
> 1980.'

Vaguely curved
horizon, white caps (some of these turn out to be seagulls), breakers,
surfers between the flags – one just fell off his board – and a dirty
textured sand beach. Apple-green dustbin with two sharp ridges, a faint
ridge and rounded lip – partly rusted; and behind this, Norfolk pines,
a white railed path, slope of interconnected grass root systems, rock
inscribed FOSSIL SUCKS, power lines hung down to two-toned green
lavatory/changing shed (half obscured), and the rock ledge with rectan-
gular swimming pool. In front of all this about 30-40 people move with
varying degrees of grace towards and away from the water.

Ken's gone to work in Wollongong
nobody else is awake yet. It's 8.23.
I'm sitting at the living room table
looking down the coast at the tankers
& smoke plumes at the 'Gong
sun glares on the back of my neck
the tin roof starts to make noises
like a leaky shower . . .

lean back (out of the sun)
bright orange nasturtium flower in a milk bottle

tracks out all over the sea – it isn't 'trackless'

that Géricault painting where the stairs to the
ruined tower must be about 2/3 the height of
the humans pushing the boat off

white chooks downhill near the cliff

it's the drinking season

move seat away from the window – it's too hot

                THUMP
                – a pile of books

as the sun hits them
postcards fall off the walls

It's better than working in a sweat shop

Blue Hills 14

A big football full of air
presses out as the wind presses in

walks up the street
eats banana & grit

past the furniture shop painting –
white rhomboidal table escapes perspective

man in neckbrace with
halfmast pants.

No mail today (threatening letters
from READERS DIGEST ORGANISATION)

the head bounces up & down
full of words. Buy shortbread biscuits.

Collect magazine from newsagents.
Phone sickness excuse to the library.

A bag full of funny gas
gathers itself on the pavement.

Poem

Looking out over the beds of tram lines
asphalted in the early 1960's thereabouts
– the woodblocked roads of 1917
& their holiday processions –

I spill tea on a T-shirt
so there is a brown stain on my heart
& the fibres of the lungs come apart
in the autumn air, looking north

at a landscape I have to be content with,
changing every few kilometers;
knees hunched in public transport
or walking instead, tracing a canal

where the only evidence is a bent lane
and a sign. My mother is a gold ring
and the design of the back of my hands.
I sell old books for new space

where lack of it means clothes on the floor
waiting for an iron & a hotel visit
to hear a band or smile at a battle
engineered by a movie company.

Pastoral Poems

1

The sky reflects the wilderness.
There are miles on the map without
                              'interesting features',
the blank spaces Dorn talks about
& which are usually somebody's home;
places I know nothing of
                              save those blanknesses,
colour of highways, unfathomables
suggesting more from less.

                    A kind of geography
which isn't, finally, a nationalism
– isn't a wallchart for a mining company –
announces there's more out there
                              than we can take in.

2

Clouds hang at high altitude.
A tin windbreak shelters a rotating sheep.

Figures group and regroup against the gust,
suit collars turned up in the spring air

an hour away from the capital
in the town where the poet bought groceries

whose books you could recognise birds from.
Outside the church, wedding guests gather;

dots on the map, imitating Brueghel
and a distant notion of the picaresque.

A pile of green logs near the station
treated with a foreign substance

await dispersal, assembly of stockades,
invented landscapes in distant suburbs.

3

Gay sailboats & bloodless nudes
                    in Art Deco bathtubs;
a vision of country 'progressives'
lumbering the 1920's into the '40's;
war poetry of urgers and speculators
in a district where a river winds
                    sluggishly to coastal lakes
– this notion of style, though rare,
aligns with the golf & polo clubs
& does not postulate Italians or Chinese
in the gardens of Wy Yung or the hills
                    round Bullumwaal
– Billy Ah Chow's now empty shack
                    near the summit of Nugong;
the last photo of him in overalls
at the Blue Duck Hotel, fifty years back.

4

Dark edged piano
in a badly lit room;
the concern with tone;

a likeness now visible
between the white folding screen –
summer japonoiserie – and this:

rhombus of sunlight
on an 18th century ornament;
the sky outside painted in 1946.

5

The young man, whom they called
'frighteningly close to genius'
moves easily in his role
among Edwardian furnishings.

An alter-ego, he is 'taken up'
because of an adjectival facility
& a bohemian facade – his books
widely praised, seldom discussed.

The drug 'experiments' prove marketable.
He moves to an ancestral dome
where wealth and imagination fall apart
in a district noted for its cheese.

6

Across a saddle from Mt Ainslie
looking northeast over open tableland
– pine plantations mark the border between
                    here & Bungendore;
a dirt road cut off by the forest's edge.
Behind, the triangulation with Majura &
                    Black Mountain,
an environment of campus suburbs
– no more than an address for notions
                    of Human Endeavour.
A tourism of sorts continues
in foreign landscapes where light is mud
& the young men (mostly) pick over
brown artefacts in green fields:
what they call 'identity'
                    a failure of imagination.

Three Found Poems

1. EVENING OF ENCHANTMENT [1973]

April Courtenay, after having tea with her godmother, suddenly finds herself involved with a gang of mods and rockers on the sea-front. From this dangerous position she is rescued by Valentine Trefusis, engaged on secret work for the Government. Just after this incident she meets Oliver Glover, who wants her to marry him and yet seems to prefer Magnolia, the friend with whom she lives. April's teenage cousin Doris complicates matters by falling for Valentine and then making trouble for him; then she gets hold of Oliver and things become still more involved.

2. ANNA [1977]

Anna is a daughter of the professional classes. Her mother is a doctor and she went to a girls' boarding school and studied art. She is nineteen and firmly in the throes of kicking against her background. She lives 'in a working class area where the people are genuine', in an apartment with a lot of other people. 'When my pictures appear some of the boys put them up in the bathroom! That's the bird . . . you know . . . the bird who does the modelling thing!' Anna is tiny, built beautifully in proportion, with a warm skin which goldens quickly under the hot sun. We are in Corfu, eating a late afternoon snack under a blue and white striped awning, blue as the Adriatic itself, watching the lobster cages stuck in the shallow water where the waiters roll their pants up and wade out to select your choice. Anna wears tight-fitting summer weight jeans which hug her contours like a glove, her wedge heels accentuating her perfectly shaped rear. Two Greek policemen having a glass of wine in the corner, gaze approvingly.

3. HEARTS [1983]

It is essential that the U.S.A. standard of hygiene and inspection procedures is maintained on the killing floor and throughout subsequent handling of all offals.

The hearts shall be trimmed of protruding veins and arteries making sure the aorta valve is removed. Hearts are to be incised to enable them to be packed flat.

Each heart has to carry a clear impression of the 'Australia Approved' stamp. It is permissible to brand in ink but if a clear impression is not obtained the hearts should be fire-branded. The hearts are to be drained of excess moisture and will be packed flat with care taken to present a neat appearance, into a plain polythene lined regular style solid fibre carton 22" x 14" x 5". The hearts are to be bulk packed to 60lb net weight, it being in order to cut one heart to obtain the exact weight.

Dogs 1

A MISREADING

the ego is a social convention
foisted upon human consciousness
by air-conditioning

*

SOUTH COAST HAIKU

Rain drips through
the tin roof
missing the stereo.

*

THE BOOK OF CHANGES

The glittering palaces
are all over the Great Water.
The seven etheric centres
of the body do not help us
to fill in the dole form.

*

THE MYSTERIES

Everything happens at once.
We miss most of it.
The kettle boils over
and puts out the fire.

*

Voss

GERMAN DIES IN DESERT:
SYDNEY WOMAN CLAIMS ESP LINK

*

SHORT STORY

Kevin patted his dog 'Bouncer'
and knew, sadly, that he would
never go to Fellowship again.

*

POETRY

If it looks too much like poetry now
it may look less like poetry in the future.
Hence Logan Pearsall Smith's line:
You can't be fashionable and first-rate.

*

PLEASURES OF THE TEXT

The editor of a magazine
who denied 'authorship' as
more than a function of print
sues a parodist for libel.

Two

from
The Ash Range, 1984-1986

Part Ten: Stirling

1865, a gold rush, supposed,
  at the Haunted Stream
    – "Haunted" meaning
by Ballarat Harry (unlikely);
  by the scream
    of the powerful owl,
known to send horses mad;
  or, finally, the black water
    of a shaded river,
the Rob Roy Hill
  cutting out the sun
    on clear June days
till 1 p.m., frost
  lying undisturbed
    for a week –
a gold rush:
  no record existing
    1865 to 1882
– wind off the mountains
  and not much wood to burn
    in a green forest.
Without gold
  no-one would have gone in.

    In '82, June,
John Polick, Hungarian,
  hit the rich reefs.
    Late that year
residents felt the need of a name
  for a town considered to exist;
    70 inhabitants survived
the slump of '84.
    And I think it about time   **28/8/1885**
    for a weekly mail here.

On all sides   **23/7/1886**
            one hears the bush carpenter,
                        there is quite a cluster
at the site of. . .
            . . . Nelson. . . Haunted Stream. . .
                        . . . Stirling;
a school, tracks
            to Mt Baldhead, Brookville,
                        and the Tambo Crossing;
this, so narrow
            Jack-the-Packer's horses
                        travel single file.

Some ten miles up the circuitous and difficult by-way   **12/8/1892**
is a little mining community called Stirling. The habi-
tations are unpretentious, and save for the presence
of corrugated iron, might be those of the pristine
black. As you approach the scattered huts after the
winter sun has gone down there is something weird
and soul-depressing in the scene. The mountain sides
are steep, and it requires a sure-footed steed to carry
you into the hamlet, wherein the most important
establishment is the store and dwelling till recently
kept and occupied by Messrs John Cohen and David
Tait. Shortly after 3 o'clock last Saturday morning a
terrible explosion roused the few inhabitants of Stir-
ling from their slumbers, and it soon became known
that a disaster had befallen the hut. Edward Cohen, a
brother of John Cohen, was the first on the scene, and
he found the hut shattered into fragments, and his
brother many yards from where he had been sleeping
– a corpse. A further investigation showed that Tait
was among the ruins, alive, and completely unhurt,
though dazed by the shock. Leading to the spot imme-
diately beneath John Cohen's bed, a spent fuse could be
traced, and other proofs that an explosion of dynamite
had been deliberately planned.

Some blamed it on
          Davey the Greek, mad
                    – a garden atop Rob Roy
and a spring of pure water
          for proof whisky,
                    broken down
eight to one,
          sold in Stirling and Ensay –
                    he didn't do it;
claimed a woman was responsible.
          Rain and trampled mud
                    left the black trackers
no evidence.
          January 1898:
                    bread baked
in an old clay oven
          set the timbers alight;
                    burnt down the hotel
and the store of David Tait.

          Caesar Brideson grew blackberry,
                    elderberry,
for quality wine; Jim Bayliss
          two miles downstream
                    sheeted a tennis court
on an ants nest;
          and "Weary" Collings
                    lost two hundred pounds
on a faked footrace,
          his hired professional
                    paid up to stall.

The Stirling ladies'   **29/7/1899**
          invitation dance
                    a decided success:
songs sung at interval
          by Mrs Butcher, Mrs Tait;

and some of the gentlemen
studying "federation".
     For dancing, the day shift
        would clean up, eat,
walk over the mountains to Ensay,
    and walk back to work.
        A drought broke
stranding the dancers
    in Stirling;
        waltzes, mazurkas,
polkas and sets,
    spanned a week
        between billets
waiting out the flood.

The battery completed the work of putting through a   **25/5/1904**
crushing for a private party of miners on the 19th
April, when the boxes containing three plates were
locked down with ordinary and patent padlocks. It was
not until Wednesday, 11th inst., that Mr Spence
noticed in walking past the battery tables a piece of
broken pine upon the floor, which on closer inspec-
tion proved to be a piece of one of the wooden slips or
cleats that had been lightly tacked in the inside of one
of the boxes to keep the copper plates in position. The
broken locks had been cunningly pieced together so
that to a casual observer they both appeared secure,
but on being touched they dropped to pieces. After
making a careful search of the premises and the
immediate vicinity of the battery, which is within a
stone's throw of Spence's Coffee Palace, the constable
returned to Bruthen, without picking up even the
slightest clue to the perpetrators of the robbery.

    A town
        falling into decline
           and no-one noticing;

that the battery
                    should remain inactive
                                and the copper plates
melted, in another state,
                    before the investigation.
                                Four years later   **25/3/1908**
– Spence
            absent in Bruthen –
                        his hotel burnt down.
The origin of the fire
            is unknown. The building
                        was insured.
The standard non sequitur.
                    The roads fell to pieces;
                                Shire Councillors
challenged to ride over them.
            Only 19 recorded votes   **6/1/1909**
                        at the recent election;
the Deputy Returning Officer
            obliged to walk
                        into Tambo Crossing.
And *there is some talk*
            of a revival in mining.

Thomas Eugene Swetnam, miner, resident at Stirling,   **27/4/1910**
applied for the forfeiture of lease No 3820, Gippsland,
at present held by the New Stirling Amalgamated
G.M. Co., on the grounds of non-fulfilment of labor
covenants. He said that from November, 1908, to
March 22nd, 1910, no work had been done on the
lease. Since the lease was issued only five men had
been employed for twelve days working it.

By 1911, Messrs
            Tuckett and Styles
                        disposed of the machinery.
Davidson and Frazer,

Tambo Crossing,
            bought the roof iron;
    still to sell:
            three boilers, two engines,
                    a turbine and overshot wheel.
The whole of the plant   **18/12/1912**
        of the Hans Co.,
                secured for £300
    by Mr Severs of Ballarat
        who put up immediately
                sundries,
    realising over £320,
            retaining most
                    of the heavy machinery.

What used to be the prosperous mining centre of   **16/1/1919**
Stirling has now practically passed into oblivion. At
the present time there are only three families residing
at the place. Some years ago Stirling possessed an
hotel, wine saloon, three stores, butcher's shop, bil-
liard room, rifle club, football club, athletic club and
cricket club. Now the place is deserted. At the present
time the machinery and plant at the Governor-
General and other mines is being dismantled, while it
is likely that before long the last public building (the
Mechanics' Hall) will also be removed. We under-
stand that the trustees of the hall are anxious to
dispose of the library, which contains somewhere
about 600 books, while they are also desirous of selling
the hall, seeing that the building and its contents,
which include a piano, are liable to be destroyed by
bush fires.

Disastrous fires are raging round Stirling. On Satur-   **23/1/1919**
day the battery known as Spence's was destroyed. A
weatherboard house and contents was also totally
burnt.

62

The acting Deputy Postmaster General: "approved of   **1/5/1919**
the closing of the post office, Stirling, as from the 30th
inst."

The hall at Stirling has been removed to Little River   **6/5/1920**
where it will do duty as a school.

Huts subside,
          lean with the wind,
                collapse;
the vertical and horizontal
          grow obtuse and acute;
                boards grey, then rot;
thick iron lasts
          a little longer.
                Fire and regrowth
clear the remains.
          So, Glen Wills:
                a sign in a clearing;
at Sunnyside there's nothing;
          Grant, a graveyard
                if you can find it.
And Stirling?
          The base of a chimney,
                overgrown,
in a small clearing;
          dark water,
                a wild fruit tree.

Three

from
The Epigrams of Martial
1985-1987

I xxv

Give to the nation
          this book
    shaped and polished,
that may stand the rarefied wind
          that sweeps eagles
    over the Black Mountain
and the flickering light where scholars
          delve amid dust
    in basement stacks.
Admit your own fame
          with no hesitation;
    its reward for your care
that these passages, alive beyond you,
          flourish now:
    glory is lost
on an urn of ashes.

I xxxvii

You drink from crystal
          and you piss in brass;
it's the vessel between
          that lacks class.

I lxviii

Whatever John does, Julie is always
              on his mind.
In the most bizarre circumstances
    John talks of Julie.
Julie is all; without Julie
    there is dumbness.
Accidentally he writes to his dad
    'Dear Julie. . . .' Julie?

Julie reads these lines and laughs.
Then John reads them, angry
    because Julie has seen them.
But which Julie am I talking about, John?
    And which John?

I   lxxii

Borrowing a poet's name O'Connor
you think yourself a poet;
a set of dentures
might call itself a smile.

II   xii

Your sweet breath tells me
    you gargle
when you don't gobble.

III   xviii

Your asthma has won
    the audience's sympathy;
don't lose it by reading
    your poems.

IV   lxv

The one-eyed
shed fewer tears.

V lxiv

'Make it a double, Johnny
. . . on the rocks . . .'
My fedora tilts.
                    Ray Charles
sings on the jukebox 'I can't
stop loving you.'
                    'The same again?'
'Same again.'
The Great Dead look benign
on whisky labels,
but I'd rather look through a bottle
than be stuck on the outside.

VI xlviii

Your after-dinner speech was flat . . .
except for the flatulence.

VII iii

If you haven't been given
a free copy of my book
it's because I don't want
a free copy of yours.

VII iv

Those about to die young,
        the insane, the criminal,
they encourage them all
            to write poetry.

VIII   xx

Dransfield, who wrote
      200 poems each day,
was wiser than his editor
      who printed them.

X   v

Let whoever has wounded respectability with verse
walk alone through the city,
exiled from lit rooms,
begging grey crusts from bag people.
Unroof the bus shelters,
brick up the archways,
have him lick the rime from his lips!
Let him think those buried
            in nameless graves
are the fortunate ones,
and in his own last hours
let him fend off mongrels
            and carrion birds.
Nor let death end his punishment:
suspend him in purgatory
wearying out centuries of torment,
and when he is driven to confess the truth
let him howl, barbed by his own conscience:
            'I wrote it!'

XI   xvii

Not all of this book is for late night reading;
some of it goes well with a hangover.

XII   lxix

Your friends,
like your *objets d'art* ,
are 'genuine antiques'.

Four

1986-1994

Blue Hills 19

Above the Mitta, the hump
      of Mt Wills;
a motorbike groaning
across the dip behind tin huts.
      At Glen Valley
a hippy couple corner onto
      the main road,
reluctant to wave
to a man in a hire car.

*

North of the knob: Sunnyside,
of which nothing exists
but black diagonal shadows
on a white road.

*

Across the border:
      Patterson's Curse
         (the Banjo?).
At Jingellic, the Bridge Hotel;
the Murray flowing a hundred yards outside the window.
The river, a 'brown god'?
    (try saying it with a Frank Muir accent)

The pub's chilling machine cuts out
and the jungle leaps in
(the publican and his father
    go up the river

and I go down a little
    to Dora Dora.

All Blues

From Boston comes the message:
      Go for it
then throw it away.

If it makes you glow
      eat it
then beat it.

Your life is a new address book.
Your visa is almost done.
But the pilot light burns in your kitchen
      all night long.

Five Spot

Monk's Coming
on the Hudson's
about appropriate
for breakfast.
White frost. Trains
in the clear air.
Discrete piano notes.

                    Outside,
sharp red berries,
grass shoots in the mud,
waiting – ghost moon
in a blue sky – for words.

Dogs 2

Proposed Host Centres for the Next Ten Annual
Meetings of The American Post-Structuralist Congress

Synecdoche, N.Y.

Metonymy, Ind.

Parenthesis, Ga.

Trope, Ky.

Phoneme, N.Dak.

Logos, Tex.

Glyph, Neb.

Mise en Scene, Ida.

Asymptote, N.M.

Closure, Nev.

*

Plastic Laurels

It's hard to make Consumerism
the hero of an epic poem
unless you're a fundamentalist
from the retail belt.

*

On the furthest mountain
the school excursion

*

Monetarism is the capitalist parody of Marxism.

*

A Space (for Gael Turnbull)

Pretending to concentrate

is distracting enough.

*

A neoclassical painting:
Minimalism surrounded by Theory.

*

At the sea's edge
depilation sets in.

*

The Fortunate Isles
ruled by junta.

*

Creative Writing

No in-
tuition
in tuition.

*

The Romantic Desk Calendar

When the Muse comes late
check the use-by date.

*

The Shorter Nigel Roberts

a bard
aboard
a bird

*

Baby Poem

grin
& puke

At Rapallo

Sun rises over San Ambrogio.
Small terraces and chapels glint in the hills behind Rapallo;
a town landlocked between rail tunnels.

From a dirt road,
                    the Sal al Pianello descends;
its rock steps,
                    piano keys, buried vertically.
Smell of woodsmoke and burnt rubber from a garden
                            down in the Via Aurelia,
and the Torrente
                    clear over smoothed pebbles
meets a mud canal at the Via Trento.

Palm Sunday in the Giardino Ezra Pound,
fishermen slice apples into sugar tubs.
Masts shadow the waterfront.
Sun flares on the Ligurian Sea
                    then drops behind the breakwater.

At night the moon is almost full over San Ambrogio,
and old women in furs
walk fluffy dogs on the promenade.

Crossing Aragon

Around Morte La Nieva
rocks and soil break through the scrub,
terraces of loose stone with no apparent crop.

Near Caspe, the Ebro is sandy and shallow, choked with yellow slime;
the earth cracked beneath green flats.

Road signs point across the river to Huesca, Teruel, Lerida,
as apartments rise from the rubble of '36.
The place was always a frontier;
      'Caesar Augusta' corrupted to Zaragoza;
its over-ornate church
      stylish as formal cruelty:
the product of obeying distant orders.

Monday after Easter, monks, hooded, in black and white robes
beat drums and blow bugles in a death march out of Goya;
haul crucifixes up a hillside
                  near the site of Bilbilis,
the birthplace of Martial, who lived in Rome,
and wrote often of simple life in the provinces.

In Perigord

Fern shapes in rock;
                              sponges
solidified in fluctuating neon;
                              human digits
scattered across gravel;
                    shapes of the Bear,
                              the Antelope;
glass bowls,
          amphoras.

                    A courtyard of broken inscriptions.
Mosaic floors from the old Roman town
Vesuna
              where children circle on bicycles
a tower split open down one side;
horseshoe of sky at the top.

The church bells toll:
          'Tote dat barge,
                    lift dat bale'
for an invisible celebration,
a tricoleur and makeshift dais
          erected in the empty plaza.
Snatches of marching music, an amplified voice:

              un   deux   trois   quatre
                  un   deux   trois   quatre
              ici
                ici
              un   deux   trois   quatre
                  un   deux   trois   quatre
                      un   deux   trois   quatre
              ici   ici   ici
                ici   ici   ici

and an old man in khaki,
weighed down by enormous red epaulettes,
steps out of a public lavatory.

Mont Ségur

Yellow lucerne fields outside Toulouse.

Mirepoix, a small walled town.

At Lavelanet, a disused merry-go-round in the main street,
      the Christmas lights still overhead.

Directly south, towards Spain,
the blue form of the chateau,
                Mont Ségur,
its keep, an arrowhead
         filled with rubble from a broken well;
the Cathars seven hundred years gone.

White Saint Barthélémy shines
            through a broached wall
above the village of Mont Ségur;
a sharp drop from the battlement,
the clear sound of a rivulet,
               and further,
mountains on mountains: Pound's Cathay.

A cuckoo hoots in the valley.
Purple flowers bud at the base of the chateau.
Lizards, black slugs and small brown snakes
     stir in the equinoxial sun
immune to decrees of Paris or Rome.

The road twines through summer pastures
to the village, an ochre amphitheatre
           empty at midday.
Cowbells ring in the streets;
a faint odour of sweet shit
hangs in the restaurant.

The Front

I

The balloon-like mechanisms of reputation
hang in a barrage, gas escaping in print
and everything else consigned,
                              as though the whole tent of it
would blow away,
but the struts are no more real, the measures of what is politic
as insubstantial as clouds,
                              a civilization that could shut down
when the power is cut.

                    Here, the stone wall
runs for miles, defining a sea;
sand that would not define
providing instead a barrier.
                              The city was an accident,
a sport on the banks of what river?,
a collection of plate and cotton. And this place?
                                             This
has the city's back turned upon it.

                              Lights hung upside down once,
along the road headed for the water
where the trams fell away at night
in a murk of razors and greenish limbs;
where a curved horn, blown by a black man
            was an imagination of Harlem;
where the garish light of hotels serrated across the promenade
                    became the East River,
and the caps of sailors thrown at the heavens turned to stars.
                    Money owns it
as it once did, altering the image
to suit a popular conception: cast iron pastiche.
                    What hope for the can of 7-up
until the new interior decorator arrives?

The water is no more constant,
it reflects a prevailing imagery,
as poetry narrows and widens its trousers
out on the pier, by the rehabilitated kiosk.

2

From the Junction, tramlines ran straight towards the pier and the Catani
gardens. The last railway station bisected this stretch, where Grey ran up
to Dalgety and over the hill to Barkly; spire atop a medieval village whose
industry was flesh. Gulls circle the 'forty-five' flats and cries go up into
the night air from Luna Park, its maw, and that of Private Joseph Leon-
ski, U.S. army, who killed one because 'she twittered like a bird', killed
two others, and Violet McLeod

      lay dying in full view
      of Harold Wilson, working man,
      Victoria Avenue;

mud on the Private's boots identifying with local soil as he lay in his tent
at Parkville.

3

Figures dance around a decayed building;
linked images
cross-hatched by ladders:
cracked green heads,
                tongues
licking up the suburb.
                   The dance
is Matisse
          but the field
                  is an insurance job
and a firm handshake
              the faces
                     interchangeable in shades,

an inscription circles

                loops into a knot

                          and runs off the field

onto a red brick wall

                a ballroom's side

        in which the dance
continues its measures,
allotting time
and 'coming attractions',
looking out over the sea,
waiting for the dancers to rise;
their luminous ankles
and jackets of weed,
the clutch of bottles, broken,
smoothed into mineral shapes.
                    Slurring
from a hotel, the image of an author
fond of clean sheets, manicured, impeccable,
joins the dance, the despised music,
                      who
had been accustomed to extended periods and over-lush cadences,
whose inkings crammed with detail
lost the form itself, a point buried in incidentals
– but he is dead and the mouth that breathed him out – inflammable,
courteous, back-biting – has a notice slapped overhead.

Paint flakes, the dancers

                    peel from walls, rain
gavottes in the streets.
                  Around the dance,
curved track of the roller-coaster,
                      its rope border.

4

Penguin Modern Painters: Ben Shahn; and Henry Moore's tube draw-
ings, figures Vesuvius petrified; these, left behind in the bungalow by an

itinerant drummer as back-payment. A room left pristine by the duo –
Mr & Mrs – he ending in a police photograph, draped beside a '57 Hold-
en near the gates of the pier. Seasonal workers floating in the city, filling
in at the abattoirs, plaiting leather belts. The comic, who slid from the
tiles. Others, nameless. These the inhabitants of One-ninety-five, drink-
ers at the Vic. and the Bleak; an archaeology of the '50's.

5

The sky moves over Williamstown
as smoke angles across Hobson's Bay;
lines let you breathe, or you fall into it;
a white stick tapping up from the salt
by those arches between shops
where two-up and the meat markets
arrange themselves over a time
and vanish
                        – as the smell of coffee
cuts off that trope. But there's space
to enter it all into. And a small triangle
of dark sky above the suggested location.
                        – hot steel
at the Works, the tyre specialist
closed; sand heaped against the shutters
some winter days.
                        – but I step ahead.
Best to concentrate on the guest house,
now obliterated, its strong wood gate
and the grandmother's balcony, children
sinking into a sofa, sniffing jonquils. The sand
mounts up; a sun-shelter on the beach
is a storm shelter when the waves
broach stone and wash asphalt,
and the Motors concrete battlement. . . . .
its tin roof. . . . .

                        – the Works are a stretch
toward the estuary, on the bend behind

a reclaimed swamp; the office
confident nineteen-thirties, the Plant
like a vast hangar; roads empty of address
flanking the south wharf and the river,
the swinging basin, Victoria Dock.
                Southwest
from the river mouth
a truckload of sailboards wait,
banners aflap, the surface, still, green,
where a yacht tilts on its keel
in a sandbar.
              Its slanted mast
cuts one diagonal across the anchorage as,
plate glass of the Bleak hit by gusts,
       The Burghers of Calais lean
             out of whack with the poles
and the curve the Bay takes en route to St Kilda.

6

Tuesday afternoon, back-streets
are given to the cats. One floats
on a crushed hedge. In Alfred Square
a white, helmeted figure, raises a rifle, leans
forward, its back scarred by the claws
of *felis tigris*, facing, over the water
a rusty container, slipping through a grid of palms,
the You Yangs distant, clear today, unconcerned.

Two decades back one read from the Town Hall podium
long lines, the smiling workers trailing down
St Kilda Road to the beach.
               A decade ago, another,
now running to fat, urged the poets
onto the streets; years later, his sign
above a coffee house in Middle Park:
          Street Poetry – Inside
                   a descent

into artefact, as yet another sits, opposite ceramics and horoscopes,
intoning:

Poems on subjects of your choice

Most of my heroes are dead
      diffident, but defiant,
the way they'd catch
      evening light on milk bottles
           becoming Edward Hopper
too particular
      for wine and cheese,
         the brackets of 'discussion'.

I want to pull up
      this bevelled plantation,
         write, say,
an area of sand
      not an old seascape
         forged
that the present should resemble the past . . .

– but enough of this real-estate Edwardian,
this 'classicism', dated as an 'all-steel' kitchen.

                        Instead

trace the limbless graffiti, its red strokes
on lavatory-green of The Met.
                Try
to argue with that.

7

Deep and dissolving verticals of light
submerge alliteration in a shallow tub
         of salt, weed, and jetsam,
and the new mob shine
with bastard similes and kind hearts,

so that we are thrown back on these

               baleful decorations, unable
to show us how to cross the road, inedible,
finally a confused wrack
in which we sink or swim.

8

Fixed ideas arrive on the beach;
as the storm falters
they disport themselves, will make
colourful patterns for art photography,
even then, fade, become one with their surrounds,
uninteresting edges to be tripped over.

So the mind makes a sequence:
freeze-frame, rusty nail in a gate,
weathered lines radiating, lost
in the whorl of the grain, the iris
disappearing to depths
beyond the back of a head

like a diagram of Garden City
and its bus routes, grey and red-brick
familiarities which make a door-knocker,
a set number of steps, some guide
to location. When streets take a semi-circle
blocks are thrown from perspective.

Hewn wood, chunks of mallee root,
brown against grey palings, carpets
of muddied sawdust, patterns in hard
concrete there for the invention of games:
hop this one, miss the lines, step on
a crack; ridges of moss on broken pipes;

old dog in a wooden box, flesh
lapping against splintering sides,
will sleep through noon, wake

when a downpipe cuts off the sun
and potplants strain forward. Observed closely
this landscape induces vertigo;

the ball spins back from New Right graffiti
to the half-cupped palm, is pitched again
and takes a tangent from a white line across asphalt,
shooting leftward over grass and nets,
and the park's inhabitants, barrelled in prams
or propped on sticks; its language. . . . .

9

'Dreadnoughts of the Tramway Board
Forge up the furious street'
                      so, Furnley Maurice.

          The city
is no more than a map, and this isolated hook
south of the river, a bay within a bay;
sets of words superimposed,
highlit, erased;
                black and white diagonals
grimy on the rail-bridge, where there's a sign, black and white again,
pattern on pattern; as wires dangle
currentless.
                The new line swings
from Clarendon up to the old,
and derelict stations cling in the air
        down to the Port.
When power fails, a bank of passengers, muted,
observe the city, its towers as promises;
flags risen beyond a bunker:
                      a glittering idea
fit for some Chamber of Commerce to sweat over,
that the suburb should twin the city, this line
a causeway across low ground,
green space marking the path of a creek;

        sludged channel
abutting where the beach at slack tide emits
weed smell,
             mussel smell.

Captain Cook stares out
        at a stretch of water he never saw;
the imagination erects one locality, government
           erects another.

It might as well be spring and all

for Rosemary Hunter

1

You can do nothing consistent.
Carnegie. Dying gums
from which 'a plate of teeth' &c.
Abandon here syntax and hope,
just be washed, with this grey linen
and keep your eye on the clock;
lamplight in this room has not yet
rendered the outside dark
or the blue glow of oil heat
sent out an aura.

2

Sharp light on serrated funnels,
the chatter of the ABC at breakfast
– why can't they be morose?
Then there's Bruce Ruxton, some fart
from the Club. But under this blue plate
Asia seems no monster;
metal frame of the window holding
a Hokusai jigsaw,
matching pencil strokes
on the bedspread.

3

The man in the neat dressing gown
has gone, his cat with him;
his rooms, painted white weeks ago
are empty, the back steps
camouflaged with leaves; only

the rooftop's population unchanged:
nodding mynas and the dart
of silvereyes among the figs.
The weather has carried off the inhabitant
and the colours of bricks are no longer
the same; rust behind the upper buds,
a lone antenna carrying nobody's image,
possums brawling on the back fence.

4

Basil clings to windows through which
there is no depth of focus
beyond a cream chimney, slanted
rooftop tanks, hanging leaves.
Worms work through soil
under damp twigs and bark chips.
Pigeons gather near the gutter
over small round pools of themselves.

5

Milky light in the hall
from a garden lamp; aspirin light
as the couple from upstairs argue
in the stairwell. Doors open,
shut, then night takes away traces.
Broad, simple outlines of fig leaves
have nothing to do with this, nor
current affairs radio: the world above water level
of milk cartons and goodbyes,
of shifting light on red brick.
And the books lose their phosphorescence,
become objects; a landscape is pieced together
from twisted articles of a language
which kids us it's older.

6

A dragonfly affixes itself, nose to the wall,
the long tail drooping; a black spider
attached to the ceiling, forms a ball;
red flattened features of a wasp, crushed
in a roll blind, lie on the windowsill.
The shower of gnats has passed; a few
stray bugs cling to the furniture, stick
to the matt of grease on the cupboard floor
where oil bottles sit; or fumble, feet upwards
amid breadcrumbs in a washbasin.

7

Sheets of tin bang in a night gust
blocks away, footsteps sound from the passage
at two, when mosquitoes descend
on the bedroom's tent. Then daylight:
everything defines itself, parodies of the normal;
light movement of branches, the gale spent,
the spread of grass on a corner of earth
mown flat, paths swept, the garbage taken away.
Things you left on the table are still there,
the plants grown an inch taller; the cool
lemons have not escaped from the refrigerator.
Out on the street a tram stops and an old man
in a purple suit and cowboy hat
climbs down and totes his airline bag
across an intersection through the dull heat.

8

The table turns on its side: a Matisse!
and flowers creep up the window
across a grey sky, pink curlicues;
a clothesline above the flats deflects

coming rain, as the west moves in.
Yellow patches of blossom grid the tree
a couple of backyards away,
vases stand at regular intervals
across an isometric plane;
the trellis cross-hatch – above this
plumbing juts into space:
round ventilator shafts, corrugated tanks,
and an overflow pipe wobbles in a gust;
curves into a question mark.

Blue Hills 21

Out at the twelve-mile mark
peppercorn seed equals memory.
A lizard flits under rubble
between the sleepers, on the line where
trains 'rocket to impossible destinations';
overhead, pale green semiconductors,
a sky full of cirrus.
                              It's spring:
the peppercorns hang, an innocent aura
of ten year olds sharing cigarettes
in a hollow of compacted earth
under the waiting room.
And the lunatic who pushed a barrow
from the station to the newsagent,
infantile in middle age, what burst gland
disposed of him?

Blue Hills 24

Half an hour down a straight road
from the prison farm, Boof Morgan sings Country
to a synthesizer, a drum machine
and a dozen desultory lovers of genre.
A man and woman mime each number
while the barman lives by reflex
metres from where the boats tie up.
Thickset men with beards and cowboy hats
gather elsewhere, under the bar T.V.
They are no friends to this music
– wear its apparel with no concern
for a pickup draped with the national flag
– departed next day from this fine drizzle
across a map of blue skies and faithless love.

Blue Hills 32

                    Layered mountains:
the nob of Ben Cruachan, sharper from the west,
blighted Mt Hump emergent for some distance.

Above Cheyne's Bridge the road swings up Hickey Creek
towards a gap; bared rock diagonal
hard under McMillan's Lookout.
                              A dirt track
skips a cutting, follows a shoulder to the point of the ridge
a few steps from the road; lichen on half-buried stone,
purple flowers in clefts.
                        Campfire ash in a small clearing,
Big Flat below, where the Macalister erodes edges of pasture;
cattle on the open ground, sheep dotted in rising scrub.

At Licola the settlement is boxed in for two more months,
its general store closed mid-week.
No sound or movement here, save a chain-saw
somewhere across the oval.

Blue Hills 37

white masts
dense hail

a pale blue band over Williamstown
fix of the Westgate Bridge

seagulls huddle and peck
at twigs, without option

a man carries a sign
over his head down the pier

Untitled

Not to assume a mantle,
not to have you look so closely,
I refuse to be explicator;

instead, a wanderer
in a landscape prefigured
trying not to bend its edges

with that ease that wraps
a thing around itself
like a slumming majesty

out arraying the dirt, the glitter,
its personality, preferring instead
to leave a smile

suspended between trees like a hammock.

West   *(i.m. Ed Dorn)*

> I stumbled along with the most wicked grin of joy in the world,
> among the old bums and beat cowboys of Larimer Street
> — Jack Kerouac

On the Best Western bus
– a guy with iguanas in his bag.

*

At breakfast, a cowboy tells the cashier:
'I'm pretty sure that's not the design on my tie, I think I dribbled'.
The accents out here differ from the midwest twang;
the place slower, though no less businesslike.

The Boulder bus skirts the edge of Denver
– its streets deserted, Friday after 9 a.m. –
traverses a wasteland of metal bridges and factories;
toward the Rockies, a sign: STORAGE TEK;
in the smooth fawn hills, rows of bunker-like structures.

*

Motel rooms may have all the 'homely' aspects in the world, but you can
never quite belong in them. The furniture suggests uses it will never have,
the utilities are, like the politesse of waiters, threats of extortion.

*

Up Pearl Street for coffee in the cool air.
Indian corn, orange pumpkins and all things wooden
fill the windows of a yuppie shopping mall.
Pinball palaces silent under the Rockies;
the main street vacuum clean,
within touching distance of the mountains.

West across a canyon, the first of the steeper ranges
– the Rockies proper – covered with snow. South of Boulder,
the 60° angle of the Flatirons, Table Mesa.
A large installation tests 'atmospheric conditions',
monitors winds, connects somewhere to star wars.

Rainy night. In the Mexican restaurant bar – as everywhere else in town –
the 16 year olds try to get drunk.

*

I go down 28th for breakfast at the Last American Diner – a chromium
masterpiece with waiters & waitresses on roller skates. Pack & walk up
to the bus terminus on 14th & Walnut. En route for Denver, notice that
last night gave the front range (beyond the foothills) a coat of snow. In
Denver get a cab to the Regency Best Western. My room, on the 10th
floor, looks over industrial waste – the South Platte River buried in there
somewhere – probably a putrid creek at this elevation – and out to the
west & southwest, the Rockies.

*

In the last 20 years, Microchip City swallowed Kerouac's town; its tall
buildings, a whole lot of them, half-empty. The big boom didn't materi-
alize, but the place has pretensions, is 'go-ahead': number 6 on the 'most
likely' list. The charm is its failure to measure up.

Across the tracks, over the river, Denver goes Mexican.

*

Downstairs in the Stuff'd Shirt Bar – the TV news.

Provinciality measures itself by the degree to which role models – TV
announcers &c – approximate to the metropolitan ideal: the accent
mightn't have the same sharpness; the fashions date a little – but a strain-
ing towards the model is always perceptible. The 'cast of thousands' com-
mon to contemporary news programs complete each other's sentences
– in the process denying the 'personality' they presume.

The languages of America are seductive. It's a pleasure. But maybe it's more so because it comprehends a limited duration.

The prevalence here of cowboy hats.
And the stretching of vowels: 'The house shar-blee.'
Someone asks for a doggy bag for drinks.

I think I like the west a lot.

One for the room.

The barman answers the phone: 'Stuffed Shirt?'

*

The cab driver, a WW2 vet, ex-postmaster,
reckons his C.I.A. file is an arm long (anti-Vietnam activities).
He figures Reagan has been dead some time
& what we have up there is some kind of robot.

*

Union Station is filled with railroad memorabilia
– the rail, ceasing to be functional, becomes an 'experience'.

'You must have shoes on at all times while travelling in the train.'

*

The chief steward is called 'Noel, that's K.N.O.W.E.L.L. … I wear my Amtrak identification badge over my heart – where it should be … and I walk numinously down the train.' As the journey progresses, Noel turns out to be a pain in the ass. At regular intervals the P.A. gives out a fake old-time engine whistle before his recitals of geological litanies in language even a moron could understand.

The train winds up the foothills & crosses the continental divide 9,500 feet up, in the Moffat Tunnel. Somewhere behind me in the compartment, a 22 year old woman & an old man discuss human nature endlessly.

In the evening we enter Utah through Ruby Canyon. I dine with a young gay from Salt Lake City ('Are there many gay people in Australia?') who spills his salad dressing; and a good humoured black woman from Cleveland. When he describes life in Salt Lake, its restrictive liquor laws &c. then talks of the large size of Mormon families, she says 'At least they're doin somethin right'.

*

Wake up around four or five, Pacific time,
watch the saltbush of Nevada grow light after Winnemucca.
Sparks & Reno, 8-8.30 a.m., the poor man's Las Vegas;
then up into the Sierra Nevada and down slowly to Sacramento
– mullock heaps still visible in the mountains.

Across the American River the country flattens
       – flood plains all the way to Martinez
       (home of Joe DiMaggio, John Muir, & the martini).

The East Bay houses a mothball fleet
and the largest importer of Japanese cars;
the bombs that fell on Pearl Harbour
       were made largely of U.S. scrap metal.

Chicago

rails sit on the ground
and the frame houses
beside the line stretching to Omaha
the tall buildings an empty boast
on a lake of empty boats
loading up for the Erie Canal

Outside Eugene

Light differs
as though morning persists

dried grass, bleached flowers
pieces of cracked china

a graveyard amid
truck farms draws together
a network of hamlets

red and yellow pumpkins
bright in packing cases
three weeks to Halloween

At Jonathan and Tom's

Rowan berries cluster;

long shadows of stone fences ride
up Dentdale's side,
                              the Dee
circuitous below Corn Close.

Miles above Sedbergh,
amid fells that felt
the glacial rub,
                              sheep high on the slopes
delight
in the light.

Ornithology

So far and no safari
— Mark O'Connor

An invisible neighbour dumps a box of plants in the backyard.
It rains softly over the town.
Art Blakey
has just played 'Moanin'
a favourite from 1958
but I've removed my headphones
to see in May of 1993

a service today for Bob Harris,
which John attended – without Martin Johnston's 'In Memoriam'
(buried in my cache of poetry, somewhere in a box labelled Tampax
up the road at Jenny's place.

I imagined Jas Duke
playing chess with Martin: they would have found community
though they never actually met.
Bob, Jas and Martin: all to some extent
'self-educated' – or at least
(in Martin's case)
'eccentrically' educated.
But Bob didn't
(as far as I know) play chess,
and wasn't a lover of knowledge for its own sake.
He was more directed,
funnelling all things into poetry.
Jas could tell you about the I.W.W.
or the American electoral system;
Martin, anything
you'd want to know about Greek-Turkish conflict
or poets imprisoned by the junta.
Jas would recite my poems.
He knew them better than I did
– *his* concern
not *my* bad memory.

That I couldn't locate

Martin's poem for John

due to our interior rearrangement

– books elsewhere, except for a few odd titles,

the hall piled with junk (what useful things become

when shifted to inaccessible locations

– a creaking metaphor

for our lives' rearrangement, distantly

though importantly

by these dead poets.

A young lawyer moves into Lisa's vacated flat.

Rudi appears more ravaged, who walked

– a young Czech – back from Stalingrad

without shoes, to Germany in 1943.

And I write

in the kitchen with my second beer; the living room

as yet uninhabitable.

Rosemary walks the wooden floor in search of books with answers

amongst what remains of our references.

A green Olio Sasso tin

empty, on the kitchen floor,

smell of turpentine outside.

I hold a shell to my ear

to 'hear the sea'

I hear Germans or Swedes next door

the steady rain not conducive for Eurotravellers' activities

a wall of cartoons before me, faded, brittle,

to be replaced by more recent follies.

I think about Art

– Art Blakey, that is,

and the Jazz Messengers –

and Jas, Martin and Bob:

their notions of art about as various as it's possible to be.

I remember once

John and I, criticising Martin's long poem

'To the Innate Island'

noting (to his chagrin)

this sort of poem couldn't be written anymore
                    (the poem with a whole culture as its burden)
                              but he'd written it, and
                    there it was, and is.
          Younger, we were not aware
                    how deep the cut would be.
                                        And now the poem exists;
          a construct which gives pleasure
                                        and gives the lie
               to notions otherwise expressed
                              applauding the 'vernacular republic'
                    – John said of *that* one it implied
                              'the kingdom of proper usage' was elsewhere.
          We wished to escape these handy apothegms,
                         write *what* was possible
                                             as it was.
          I blow my nose with a red handkerchief, cook dinner,
                              pour another beer,
                                        ease into this May evening;

the imagined and impeccable response of Ken Bolton and John Jenkins:
                    'Very well sir, it's your poem
          and you must include what you wish sir.
               I sir, desire only to obtain the bird.'

                              Yeats said: a poet
               'is never the bundle
          of accident and incoherence
                    that sits down to breakfast.'

                              Yeats was a shit.

The Indian summer is over,
                         leaves of the fig only beginning to yellow.
          I'm happy we don't have real seasons
                    – the sight of all that dead vegetation
                              between Washington and New York

last year's fall,
and what a relief it was
to get to San Francisco
and the green of eucalypts:
not simply a sense of being
closer to 'home'.

Groan of a tram from the Esplanade.

A dirty wind

distant radios
turpentine
the Triffids singing
'Chicken Killer'.
Tambourine Life!

I punch holes in the mystery bags
– in the mixed metaphor of political commentators
'puncture a few sacred cows'

Buried items:
my guitar
with blackened bass strings.

I couldn't understand why older people owned musical instruments
they no longer wished to play
– were these the discarded apparatus of courtship?
(for me, simply the knowledge that imagination
exceeded physical capacity
and I would never be able to play the tunes I 'heard'
– this and a hatred of the 'folkie' strum.
I would want to make an acoustic instrument sound electric;
play against its limitations

– of a piece I guess
with my feelings about poetry;
no wish to condone a limited and sectional interest
in its workings.

Works of the past remain great even if we venture elsewhere,
they're taken for granted if used as templates

                                        and I always suspected
                    the search for romanticism's narwhals
                            – why not the washing machine?
            the sausage?
(The Mystery Bags of Charles Péguy!)

A pair of shoes sits in an upended bookshelf
            – the place where 'In Memoriam' should be?
                    I catch the light rail to escape from paint,
pass the lit windows of pubs, cars streaming home
                    after peak hour, a lovely choreography;
                    the restaurant (changed name, changed cuisine)
        where I was first led to meet Rosemary's parents
                            – a mysterious 'older man'
                                    (= 'trouble')
                    though I was still in my thirties.

                        The rail passes into blackness after City Rd
        then the towering lights of this (so they say) sick city.
                    Cross the north end of Exhibition Gardens to Lygon St
                        where I buy a book about American punk music.
        At the University Cafe we dine with two lawyers.
            I nod off during a long argument on the inequity
                                    of rape sentencing;
                        imagine I'm with a bunch of medieval scholastics
                            investigating form and matter.

Scatter newspapers and items over these floorboards
                                    while there's still space.
                    Pick out a rough blues
                                    the guitar strings
            holding some kind of tone still.

Metallic sky at 4 pm over Chapel St,
    a line of used refrigerators,
        grey over the art school

        'little fidget wheels' &c.

Water slips down gum leaves,
        pools and drips from fig.
                Friday.
        A wrong number.

I get up to see what happens next.

        A foghorn.

    Pigeons wheel over a rooftop laundry.

Remember when the avant-garde writers would sit around
    describing the items on their desks?
        (If I buy a set of spanners
                will I become a mechanic?)

    Television squares the reflection of this couch
        into a few centimetres;
                stretches it vertically
so that my legs, in the middle, break the screen
        in a dark stripe like a Barnett Newman
    (so *who* said: 'aesthetics is for the artists
    like ornithology is for the birds'?
                Ad Reinhardt?

    Dancing laundry

    a gust of rain

mahogany on pale hardwood
                (sneeze)
    'implements in their various places'
another gust (the sky: piebald?

'couple colour as a brinded cow'?

(why compare a hemisphere
to a beast?

Ask the poets.

Or I'll watch blank television
like 1976.

Birds manic at dusk
a wide-screen movie through the venetian slats.
The light that can't be photographed
behind the birch.

We are condemned to write as we please
shirts flapping against the skyline
traffic rumble downhill.

could I burn the books
(not the records!)
to begin again
not even a desk
replete with objects to describe.

I have floorboards,
a TV   (TV!)
but I won't describe the casing
– that would be too John Forbes.
To describe the cathode ray tube
would be too John Tranter
(though from this
I'm saved by ignorance).
I'd mention
the program if it were on
(being a literalist)
– tonight: The Maltese Falcon!

Now the light outside has faded
leaving the yellow of the hostel's kitchen.

It's a cold-weather sky,

Melbourne finally temperate and autumnal.

A car horn stays on for several minutes.

Somewhere in this city: a tram

with my poem on it

(two lines on a poster.

Hope the artwork's O.K.)

It's Saturday.

We buy clothes, then a mirror;

run into Jenny and Reg shopping together

(who wear the same shirts in different cities)

A side of my watch

stained yellow with varnish;

the watch dating from a trip to Adelaide and the Flinders Ranges

i.m. Charles Buckmaster

who went that way circa 1970

and wrote of Quorn and Wilpena Pound.

I never met him

(saw him working once

in the Whole Earth bookshop)

and would not

have found much to talk about, I think, till later

had it been possible.

No-one to share a sensibility with

(except maybe Ken, though our humour's a bit different

and I'm slower on my feet

possibly more lateral

– excessively

some would say.

I wonder how much this has to do

with the stroke I suffered in 1966.

It started me on poetry

– well, gave a space to begin writing in

(like a hole in the head?).

Maybe did grievous damage to my analytic capacities,

holding in suspension self-criticism

just long enough to give poetry a chance
                    and letting loose the shaping intelligence later
                                        on the idiot product
                (like a surfboard
                        lost in Peru).

A pilot light splutters in the otherwise silent kitchen
                as a clear day clouds over.
                                Rosemary, comatose, has missed all this.
A household boxed and stacked is full of possibility
        – if we could live this way forever.
                        But there are books to consult, pieces of music
                inaccessible here or elsewhere, which no-one
                        could have imagined would be necessary
                                – memory allows
        and does not allow a return to beginnings
                (brain-junk can't be disposed of so easily
                        so a use must be found for these pieces
                apostle spoons, odd socks and vanished riffs,
                        my old school motto: *Labor Omnia Vincit*
(that futility, a prefabricated set of classrooms
        on Melbourne's (then) outer edge
                        with a latin tag.
                We were mostly office and factory fodder
                        harbouring a few right-wing councillors
                                (owners of slide-rules).
        Monash Uni up the road was a different matter:
                the Labor Club brought new levels of boredom
                        – my first experience of the 'procedural motion'.

In 1968 I would not wear jeans
    – a phenomenon I saw as the upper class dressing *down*
            (the 'boss class' as the Labor Club would say).
                I wanted to dress *up*
        wore black and white check trousers and neat turtlenecks
                like my favourite bands.

Years later, long haired, bearded, in flared jeans
        I appear on the right of a photographed group:
                        Kris, Retta, Robert and others with Robert Duncan;
        an inner-city backyard,
                                        Duncan having read
                with metronomic hand
                                                the beats between words
                                                        just as important,
                        and listened
as we read portions of our own work,
        taken in particular by Walter's poem
                (Walter Billeter).

                        I look all this up in old diaries
                                – but I didn't keep one in 1976;
                my poetry notebook
                        filled with intermittent scrawls,
        the writing getting larger and less decipherable
                at the end of drunken nights.
                        Still no mention of Duncan's visit;

        just the photograph
                on the wall at Collected Works.
I had been in Melbourne a few months;
        interviewed in a pub
                for a teaching job.
                                        I taught for a whole semester
                                                then drove back to Sydney
                thankful for sweat and alternative radio
                        (Unemployed at last!).

        I didn't write about the things on my desk,
                I drew pictures of them:
                                                crooked chair backs,
                        jars of pencils, book spines.
                        I would copy labels,
                                items from newspapers,
                        misread headlines.
        In the library I would investigate Chinese texts,

articles on geomancy
and their bearing on the siting of cities
– this was 1977:
Alan Wearne
in Sydney, with John Forbes
held up a newspaper headline:
the death of Elvis
in Victoria Park
(the headline, not Elvis)
– just beyond the library
where I ferreted that year
salvaging from the stacks
items on popular culture of a city in wartime and depression,
the culture of Luna Park
remote as Borobudur and Angkor Wat
through which my father (still in uniform) walked;
a set
for an unmade movie
– 'snippings of idiot celluloid', not
The Maltese Falcon –
a jumble of genres
when backyards of the poor were allowed
to abut on the Harbour
and in Melbourne the rich had no interest
in Port Phillip Bay . . .

. . . choppy, under cloud,
the horizon clear to the Bellarine Peninsula
as I round the Upper Esplanade
heading for Acland St and music
(the abrasive notes of Link Wray
reverberating later
in the emptied living room.

Mauve and silver tonight,
a red beacon intermittent
over towards the rip
as I round Alfred Square to the bottle shop.

Return to a floor coated with fine powder,
              walls patched with white
                        round the window, uncurtained,
       aquarium-like;
              slump on a couch before the television
                    feeling rigorous
                          in a sloppy way.
              The Selected Martin Johnston
                              (John says) including prose
                    to appear next month
                          (will there ever be a collected poems?).

                              We would taunt Martin
                    with his prized pentameter
       'polychromatic springtime's gay cadenza'
                          recited in race-callers' tones.
              Martin, I remember mostly
                    weaving, snake-like at a table
                          barely able to stand
                              voicing his poems perfectly.

This evening turns wretched.
       In cold rain I wait for a rail to Fitzroy,
              step off in Johnston St for a restaurant
                                    but before this
                    into the Tankerville
              where Vince Jones sang,
                    Wilbur Wilde sitting in
       – the band's slightly raised eyebrows
                    as he played at Charlie Parker,
       a rock'n'roll honker out of his depth
              (his spacings meaningless
                    unless as pause for the next idea.

Painted on the bar walls,
              a Greek god
                    with muscles twined like macramé.
       Then there's a figure like Toulouse-Lautrec at a funeral
              a bottle of evil purple liquid
                    poured over his top hat

by the figure (presumed) of The Artist;
this scene overlooked by a goddess with misshapen breasts;
the whole, a kind of pastel psychosis
above the dado, the familiar tiles,
the wood floor's perspective in the long bar
rendering the pool table as a stage prop from Van Gogh.
Brett Whiteley would have been outpaced here
by naïveté's greater ambitions.
The painting's unfinished,
a segment of wall breaks off from this narrative
indecipherable without a key.
Is it still in progress?
Or was it abandoned years ago when the artist
enlisted on the other front
(i.e. joined A.A.)?
Over all this, Channel 9's quiz programs proceed uneasily
high on a bar T.V. in the grip of the Gods.

Blue Hills 44

So much of a city
is light on stonework, woodwork;
demolition turns us into archaeologists
using the maps;
                    memory,
a particular daub of colour
there, to the right,
of that mountain down the street.

Poem

A grand piano
half-buried under
a mound of straw
is part of a sentence
translated wearily
into sculpture; an idea
suggestive, as a replica
is not (which tells only
of physical effort
and entrepreneurial skill
(where the wrecked piano
came from, was it intact
or aged in situ,
what devices secured
these elements in position
and who cleared the space
around this fragment
from a barn). It's
the Surrealist's problem:
imagination shifts
its objects, not
the fork lift (so the century's
most 'radical' avant-garde
lent itself immediately
to advertising.

The minutes

The very rigid mental image of a sequence of words, just as one is taking one's socks off to go to bed, is like a view of mountains from an aeroplane. They lie there making a single, complex but comprehensible shape, with folds in them. But one hoards the sense of distance for fear of being lost if one were down there amongst the verbs and other difficult parts of speech.

– Stephen Spender

1

I ought to be able to read the book but I can't; look instead at men shifting metal tripods near an intersection, smokers loitering outside offices. My attention's about equal to the postmodern bits stuck on the walls of . . . what? The age of graffiti is over. A tram, class W, rolls up St Kilda Road to art and a postbox. What have I forgotten? Someone's radio or mobile phone which disappears after the lights.

A tenor sax plays 'Somewhere over the rainbow' on the corner of Swanston and Bourke. It could be bad or it could be Sonny Rollins. An hour later it's the same tune delivered at around the same tempo – maybe I missed the Coltrane extrapolation bit and just caught the tail end.

Broken beer bottles and melted chocolate. Even the tram shelter slivered like the Large Glass – held together by a poster (Captain Cook by his fine layer of bird shit).

2

Change of tempo. Are my sentences shorter because I am writing in private? Before me a print purports to be the surface of the moon. I have no idea which phase the real moon has reached and I'm not about to look for it. Beneath it garbage bins line the street.

Eugen von Guerard and Caspar David Friedrich have very little in common. Von Guerard was not interested in mystical symmetries.

Now close the windows a little. And leave the books in darkness.

I can tell I'm getting old by the yellowing of books I bought new, two decades back. *The Penguin Book of Victorian Verse* edited by George MacBeth. Someone is playing an acoustic guitar in the distance. I am reading the diary of Ned Rorem. From which I mistranslated *chemin de fer* as 'burning shirt'.

Rosemary is reading *A Passage to India* and falling asleep. It is a second-hand copy of the book, in which, on the twenty-fifth page, the sentence 'One electric fan revolved like a wounded bird' is underlined. Next to it, in the margin, is a single word: 'simile'.

The cricket in South Africa. A Chinese movie about a group of actors – one a transvestite. We arrive home and both burst into imitation Peking Opera. I cook beef and snow peas as the Australian bats collapse.

In the Chinese movie someone set fire to a shirt.

3

Where the artists go, can the developers be far behind? You ruin the suburb you love. And the country turns to handcraft in your wake. Handcraft becomes Burger King. Back where we started.

I would often pass by offices imagining all the inhabitants in their official dress, believing in what they were doing. Millions of ties attesting to belief. The suit (male or female) and the notion of decorum.

The Università variations. And the vegetarian focaccia. Impossible to eat with grace. Not the results, not the methodology, just the attitude.

'A language is a dialect with an army and a navy.'

Skin loose on the roof of my mouth. The days of T-shirts. Heat this end of the cafeteria, a corner by the glass. I will become very unpopular for a month or two. Replying to all the kind letters ('we wish you well in your new job'). Batman or a big mouth on someone's chest.

A man eats ice cream and wears a map of Borneo. Here comes the postman. In that clear light peculiar to April or the beginnings of a novel.

Distant shouting voices. The smell of fermented soup.

4

De Kooning's sculpture, which I've always liked. A large metal object which looks like plasticine extruded from a clenched fist.

West wind. Opposite La Mama. Where a man on a skateboard moves along the pavement, his body otherwise motionless. Sale flags flutter. 'Scot' – a form of tax, as in 'scot free'. Euro music climbs its stairs of emotion. The ice cream truck – Tarantos – a penguin raising a cone. Three languages for toilet. Where the symbol for 'men' has arms and the symbol for 'women' doesn't.

Red lights on the third floor of a car park. Radio. Office figures at 7.30 p.m. A jumble of airwaves. Writing against the steering wheel. A voice from A1 Mining Settlement (talkback). Cigarette glow. Lights reflected off a bald pate. Golf clubs or, no, a cello. Lawyers on the way to Darwin. The dun orange leaves over car roofs. Tree, still in the middle of the roundabout. Red jackets at night, a memory of the relative darkness of different films.

Thin cloud inscriptions at high altitude. Strong gusts. The buildings at Williamstown clearly defined. Smell of hot sawdust. Hallucination? Fresh bread and papers. Tar rolled onto the road down at the junction of the Upper Esplanade. Cars flagged onto the tram tracks. Brake sand whirling behind.

A gas bottle under the arm of a man in a white coat emerging from a van turns out to be a stick of salami. Gusts force through the door. Rollerblades over dead leaves. Speculation. Not afraid of getting it wrong.

The writing in my book. The printing of my diary – where the printer refuses to do page 25. Closures. The coulisses of café windows. The hand, kissed, of a man at the bottom of the stairs, by a waitress.

Speculation, or shape. The half-familiar. Pale lipstick, like Dusty Spring-field. A man bends over a perambulator to read the menu on the door. 'Men our age' – a voice behind. So I don't know what age. Though I can guess. Only a woman of a certain age would say 'men our age.'

A jacket someone left behind, hung on the banister. A few leaves left. Pa-nurge (more of it than demiurge I suppose). An older couple hold hands across a table. But I won't try for a narrative. Just drink my coffee, pay up and be gone. 'Half of Perth is in Melbourne for lunch.'

Forty-five. And grown up. Grey and damp. A protective mild rain like Manchester. Down the road, the 'forty-five' flats: apartments erected in forty-five, or just a street number? More likely. Recover from dinner, thinking up a list of book titles.

5

MAGPIE KNEE CHEER. Bugaboo. The carved lintels of blackwood and the native animals which spelt Federation. There's barely an item in our house the German craftsman would wish to lay a hand on. 'Under electric candlelight.'

The laughing Aborigine. In a photograph by (J.W. Lindt?), then trans-formed into wood carving over a fireplace in Black Rock. Kookaburra bellows. A bed that says Good Night. And a pile of photographs and pattern books.

Elsewhere Zahalka's figures on the beach, posed in front of roped can-vas, like the one of Bondi done in the 1930s. Leah King-Smith's layered histories. Or vegetation like Nicholas Caire's out of which figures might appear. Reinstated.

A room full of dated cars. Furniture. The half-empty Swedish offices circa 1950-something; an occasional table out at sea in the middle of a floor-space which doesn't add up.

It's really not much of a Gallery – I mean the architecture, not the art. A bunker with nowhere to go, or sense of progression between its random spaces. Dead ends and double-backs. A strange office in which nobody can find their own department.

Out on the street, the headlines. Incomprehensible.

6

My Grandmother with two kookaburras (at Marysville?). Grandma divided by monkey equals outer space. Divided by money. As if, in the office, at any time, a giant potato might be parked. The clothes flap 'gaily'. A postage stamp of Edinburgh Castle obscured by postmarks.

The big green cactus says it's made in Indonesia. Its fingers hold letters and lists. Dust on the tissue box. All of this under an exploding sand dune, signed Tim Burns, January 1974. A box of postcards. Frederick McCubbin's 'Homecoming' in which the outstretched hands of the man could be holding a surfboard.

7

The radio voice of the public poet. Whose women are generic and whose men are 'individuals'. 'If Michelangelo had been straight, the Sistine Chapel would have been wallpapered' (says a poster). Dotty on two cups of coffee. Grey and maroon, colours of the 1990's. The perfect sphere of a [   ] tree. Equal sap radii. A picture window.

Blue gas flame. A sine wave. Ripple in the silence, then a filling bathtub diagonally upstairs. A picture frame – rough Afghan weave. And where is the smudge? Sinuses loosen in the draft, the moist air a heater's dryness won't dispel. Silence. A wave. And the poems, emptying themselves, of the expatriate.

Remember 1968. A pair of check pants and a flagon of sherry. Art galleries seemed the heart of bohemia. A coffee house stayed open all night. Now, not so much daggy as utilitarian.

Auld lang syne. Write it on the blackboard with coloured chalk. Read it in the anthologies. The price of . . . what? A detached tone, reverberating from somewhere. Like glass vibrating at a certain pitch. A dripping tap and a clock striking ten, up on the third floor.

Write it out of the system. This diary of specious events. Odes and Days. While I was reading Patrick White, you were reading Thomas the Tank Engine. 1968. Walking home, drunk, from the poetry reading. Crossing the railway line near the house with a stepped German roof.

Cowboy music: the reverberation. On a frosty night. In Clayton the fog hung ankle deep all down the street. A line of telephone poles. And I would colour-in maps, badly, at 5 a.m.

A figure in the bath, 1954, reflecting knees and toes. Seen from above and behind with a frilled shower-cap. Erica McGilchrist, charcoal. Arcadian linoleum. Walls painted three different colours. A car tyre, balanced across a beam, in the middle of a skylight, bean bags and a cocktail of wallpapers. No Sistine Ceiling. And a road fell away to become a footbridge, planks missing, over an open stormwater channel out on the edge of the suburbs. Newtown 1976. Clayton 1958.

Sheepwash. Blasts from the past. Old New Zealand poems from the South Island. Airborne, with a letter, circa 1986. Small presses from Providence and New Rochelle. Memos from Fremantle and South London reach me years later, lying, clogged up in winter.

Weak coffee and snowy clouds. Pills. A green book turns brown against the light. A collection of recipes, some ingredients missing. Get up to piss. One tablet six hourly. Advertisements for out of print books. I breathe into a pen top and it whistles. The wind comes off the mountains.

And is locked out of the house. Though still in evidence between the walls and the bookshelves. In the kitchen four frankfurts ready for puncturing. Half a loaf of bread. Various coloured books. 'Curious mementoes.' A striped couch and a leather jacket. No $1.20 stamps. $1.05's and 75c's with large images of dinosaurs. Send the bats to your Australian friends and the dinosaurs overseas.

'Writing that imagines it is telling the truth.' I bought no newspapers today; have hardly left the house. And now have closed the window and hear only the breath of the gas heater. ' . . . an enormous hole, in which many people had been buried.'

8

Dark days. Washing hung in the kitchen. Telling the truth about what? This heartache of a nation? This bottomless state? It could be Tasmania. Dumped by a caucus of incumbents. A snow dome of poetry. Pipe-smoking figures in a rustic shelter. A disappointing day on the Australian share market.

Politicians of the 1890's reappear transformed into stone. The mythology of law. 'A rose in Spanish Harlem' plays on the kitchen radio. Clown suit. Pants hanging on the bed-end.

Drive twenty kilometres for poetry. Then drive back. Car heater and the buzz of midday radio. Pink buds, white flowers. A bicycle park.

The next day, poetry again. A lot of it bad. 'Vision' without imagination equals stadium and boulevard. Billboarding itself. As a poem faxes its punches; spells all out. Otherwise, fiction disguised as truth, parachuting into enemy territory.

The clouds have released some rain. Try to be as prosaic as possible, even mentioning the isohyets. I am an unpublished poet, but a great one. I live in an attic and work at a tattoo factory. Pumping up the tyres. Swinging from the trees. A sand dune explodes above the bed. The wall of a factory, seen from the railway yards somewhere out west.

What I have written I have written. Pink buds, white flowers, over the fence. Intermittent rain on the dead leaves. A novel written by a retired poet, printed with a plain grey cover, the fashion for technicality. I have no life but am an operator's manual. Six people think I'm a great poet (with a grey book).

As a history changes its tenses, seeking to bring its characters to life. As alive as these simulacra? Performing their works on us as advertised. This slick haircut writing. The office was not warm so I came home. As you recede through the suburbs each view takes in its precursor, making the graffiti minute against the curve of the horizon.

9

A shaded path, gardeners repotting shrubs by the Old Physiology wall. Light on silver stacks, ducts and red brick. The genesis of a book. When I should be doing something else. Driving here to sit next to a particular window. Man in a blue jacket walking on the roof. A wheelbarrow (black, red, green and blue) labelled KELSO – white stencil imitating script.

Floor plans. A map. The imagination relocates its jungle of books and furniture every week in a different residence. Considering the route it takes down the hall and through living spaces to reach its objectives. What wall shelves History? Is Art upstairs or down? Novels in the spare bedroom, the place of the prizewinners.

'The unkilled workers.'

Under an alien government, writing as testimony. The apparachiks of a provincial capital have made the magazine their own. The stuff of it: their friends' dull odes. Bad apples. Wind doubles the young shoots, the leaves as flags.

Across the grasslands to the neo-fascist library building. Water whipped off the surface of a pond (this is no place for a fountain). Curved metal sheets, bolted secure, shelter the boardwalks around temporary classrooms. Sinuses and coffee. Synapses. The tired faces of my students. Brightness in the wind. Froth edging the lake below the bridge's span.

My foot pokes through a sock. The warmth of a room preheated. An escaped dog. Car door slam. Plug all sources of draft. Electronically lodged. The spiel of right-wing anarchists carving up the territories; government as a 'service industry.'

Rhythmic music in an unknown language. The light flies. Benin. Drive time. A temporary venue (there are no clocks in any casino). Then the man with the hat, now an expert on 'the music industry.' I shut the blinds and turn on the heat. 'The son of a circus lion tamer has lost an arm.'

10

The house of poetry. Long corridors. And then I wake up.

Throw away the sushi. Pregnant with symbolism. A bottle of vichy water dropped into a rubbish bin. Time signals, insipid theme music. Outside, the mild air, temperature dropping.

Thump in the stairwell. Road tactics. A draft from somewhere felt on the lower legs. A huge entourage of intellectuals. High stress levels. Lethal and General. The sore tooth has basically been upwards.

Owning the flying kangaroo. Floating an interest. An issue which wasn't raised. A global partner. Vignettes of munificence. Drivetime. Sinking the coffers. A mild air; sempiternal. Welcome to the Gaza Strip. When people go home from his speech.

Grace Cossington Smith's curve of the bridge. A post-card on the kitchen wall. Smudged trees on Sydney Long's skyline. Steam from a peperonata. A physically disabled man has climbed Ayers Rock towing his wheelchair on a rope.

A cook book. The lure of the South Pacific. Edging towards the volume's threaded centre. Hot plates. The ABC's ten minute grabs. Calendar – July – featuring an English seaside scene lacking in distinction.

Mapping the southern oceans. A post-card of Kurnell NSW April 28, 1770. The mariner circled, upper left on a yellow background. Marbles or some object dropped on the upstairs kitchen floor. The click of an oven cooling down.

Raffle ticket. Wyndham Lewis lapel badge: The Enemy. Hot potato. An unreasonable day.

11

The false spring at an end. Winter blossoms on wire mesh. Mussolini's idiot grandson represents things as they are. The reality sinecure. When do the concrete monuments come down?

The res publica: a cash crop. The view from an office window. A bag full of votes. And the street is bare that runs from the defunct brewery to the mausoleum. Its governing horse-mechanism fresh from policing the brothels of Saigon. This roulette Duce. Abandoned children in the car parks.

By the river's side a marine engineers' factory, built of ship's parts. A lathe the length of a liner's propeller shaft. Giant spanners. Now a layer of raked-over gravel on the site of the new monument. Brown river, no witness. The histories will be rewritten.

Printing the document: 'Women workers and the liberal state.'

The city sky's baroque, then the picture window turns dark. Green dish-washer lights. The department closed for the weekend. I drink tea and wait. Read poems written in another city. Letters of the deliberately circumscribed followed by those of an adventurer. Both of them drank a lot. Disjunctive essays. In America they go to bars to be alone. In England they go home.

12

Pigments and their dates. They look so much better as powder. Cadmium, Alizarin, dating from the 1830's; Umber and Sienna from 2000 BC. For the 1960's we have Titanium. On the white saucers they appear alchemical; on canvas, mere accident.

'A virtual reality theaterette. A post office. Some binoculars.' A double grid of venetians and branches. The Prime Minister's radio voice over a background of twittering birds. Schumaker-Levy 9 slams into Jupiter.

The Approach of the Cocktail Hour – a painting by René Magritte. The Ghost Highball in the Sky. By Jove! Grey day, yellow socks. A peevish report by Lord Peter Whimsey. Wonder what the old bastard was thinking about?

In the drawers are years. 1961 to 1988. All the atlases are out of date. There are two more minutes of light every evening. Meaning I still haven't closed the venetians on the grey Japonisme. A book from 1934 divides races up into sequential categories. Guess who makes it to the Upper Civilised?

Now it's time to pour a drink. Letting in natural light to deliver jaunty nautical feel. A small card featuring an American flag leans against the pencil sharpener. Hebraic-Melvillean Bardic Breath did not pass this way. Save it for the poetry reading, buddy!

I have increasing difficulty in reading my own handwriting. Somebody misread my signature as Lois. Lord Whimsey writes his column, bridging the gossip gap. Good News from New Zealand. The poems are on their way. Last bird calls. First call for alcohol.

The people I am singing to are dead. Harp song at evening. Underground rumble. The Link Wray version, roughed-up and plenty-where to go. If you fail to be symphonic return to the gramophone.

'Mistah Kurtz he dead.'

Thus midwinter: an American flag propped against a pencil sharpener. A small dog given orders through a megaphone.

13

Silence has a counter-rhythm, the drums, rumble of a July night. Old building songs. Floors hammered that way in 1940. Pages of gas, arcs of appliances, newspaper underlay. A wall of a hut in New England: 'Russians declare Port Arthur impregnable.' A jar of eucalyptus oil with a half-rotten label. Sliprails and collapsed corner posts.

All this was of a different latitude. It happened in the late 1970s. We approached the rise, down on the river flats and I said 'Wouldn't it be funny if there were a building over this hill.'

Which will disintegrate first – the writing or the recycled paper? Will the creases in the map split before a destination happens? At least the table is solid, not wobbly like the one outside. Constraint. No books on the subject.

The bush balladist with irregular metres read like Gertrude Stein. Thirty pages of reminiscences.

Ken Searle paints John Forbes as Zeus. In a bath towel. Who are the other gods? I can't physiognomically relate them to anyone in particular. Except Basil King as Hephaestus. Forging the consciousness &c.

Half-remembered words in Italian. Bisogna. Evidence of lacked commitment. The Florentine clock tower reads 2 pm. The tower is for sale. Forza Italia! Are Ken and Cath lost in New York? Were the great comic operas written in perfect order?

The baby parade. 'You had the baby you gotta love it.' Will yellow bricks look any better with age? Not the program, but the static. Pure radio. The Great Hulk walks down the centre of Lygon Street.

After Orientalism, Cleopatras: 'Hot and Soft Drinks.' Waiting for tawook and kebab in icy July. Hot and soft. Freezer door slam. The ingredients slowly come together. Young man reading a Penguin Classic. It's a quiet night on the Nile. Wind flaps the plastic strips. Out there in Fitzroy Street. Time to put E. Said aside. The Penguin Classic is *Heart of Darkness*.

Trombone bray. What some book referred to as 'brass truculence.' Citi Movement, New York, 1992. Saint-Saëns senseless. The book I need buried somewhere in a warehouse. Lord Boofhead and Sir Peter Whimsey pronouncing in their separate spheres.

And so, The Poems. Devolve in a springback binder. Their tacky mythology. Whose? Not mine. Personalities parade under one face. Mysterious voices which come from somewhere beyond the back of the throat. That funny theory about parts of the brain.

Now it's ruthless ensemble. Whistles in the background. When suddenly the Mardi Gras becomes the blues. That relentless piano roll. I'm on that train, despite appearances. That movement through twelve bars interrupted by a brass arpeggio. Roll on Mr River. Roll on can-opener, bright sky. Though it's dark now and I sit at the feet of an altogether . . . But I'm rambling. Six minutes into the piece. Car doors slam in someone's backyard.

Watermelon man. We begin in comradeship and jest. Later, watch the lights of a nearby city. At telephone's length. All our big serious books. This has been the life story of a male poet. Copyright © nineteen-eighty-something.

Now we're all dancing on the deck of a ship. A Ph.D in popular culture. 'What's that you're sellin?' The golden key to modern art? A sea of discourse? But who do I invoke to break the perfectly level tone? Like Hugh Trevor-Roper the imperial facade. Come as you are, without your carousel. Without a rudder.

Across the stitches, over the Divide. Sunlight breaks up the paving. The grid of letterboxes, pigeonholes. A sum of everything till now. Photocopied maps, illustrations. But the thread rising like a graph. As though a group of coloured templates slid around and created a new world. Those fragments of tree which once described a geometry. The furled lines of text abandon their disposition. Now everything is put into the cabinet of the dishwasher. A man looking like Billy Thorpe crosses the road. You step outside into the televised landscape.

And all's well. Though I believe everything I'm told. Which is liberating. The spring of the branch. A trolley full of internal mail. Blue letters on a hardware store landscape.

15

From where I am the magazines submerge and the authors go pale. The world is a better place than it was while it lasts. Depends who you are. Coffee, movies, clearing spaces. The waitress crumples an order, staring into Lygon Street. A moronic looking guy stomps his feet at an outdoor table. A Sydney writer finds me guilty of 'Political Correctness.' Sunlight on the Chinese Bistro opposite. What do I plead to the judge? Pizza box.

No more enamel writing please. Just curious happenstance. The purposive look of those on the street. The graph of windows and furniture, then sunlight. Giggle, then cover the mouth. A man with a pigtail. Waiter smoking on the median strip.

Black roofs and light after a downpour. Tiled length of the Cafe Italia, near empty. The man walks around with his mobile. Waitresses talk behind the bar in an absolutely level tone which sounds like they are reading passages from a book. About Japan. But I can't make out further details. Maybe the black and white people are all waiters? That one has left the phone on his table. Perspective of white sugar and brown ashtrays. A plate fitted to a wall: 'The sign of professionalism and integrity.'

16

A crate of oranges upset on the footpath, picked up by three passers-by. Oranges roll under cars. Nothing rhymes with orange. A man in a suit makes a left-hand turn without indicating. Nothing rhymes with orange. T for teabag, H for hat. Bring your own phone. Rooster and locomotive. Nothing rhymes with orange.

The tree in a backyard near the Safeway parking lot. A white cockatoo on a branch, talking. They have re-organised the aisles; where have the teabags gone? What logic behind placement of the soup? Steam patches on the kitchen window. Inside, a book on harems, odalisques. 96 degrees in Tampa. Newspapers over the floor. Pellets hit the windows.

Endings. A smell of hot pastry. Men in suits like schoolboys. The rear of a sign 'Sorry we're closed.' And a draft from the street. Familiarities. The coffee arrives. Closure. A handful of old telephone books, hugged to the chest. 'Shot' and 'captured' by a photographer.

A form, already set in its vocabulary. So the Language Poets think. But their conceptions are also set. We're all prisoners here (We are all Language Poets comrade!). What then? Lunch. The mention of coffee. The sense of coherence, topos (my lunch thought up at the speed of sound).

A drunk on the tram. Mr Vietnam. Smelling out the length of half a carriage. Who argued with someone else who smelt even worse and got off in South Melbourne. People vacate the window seats when others become available . . . nearly said appropriate. Still fighting Communists on the light rail to town. We function with only half the available information.

17

The Boss signals space. Packing them in. I'm behind on my reading (flipping the contents of a filing cabinet). This afternoon I'm unable to follow Sartre. Or just not interested in his disentangling of the dialectic. What about photography? Mr Sartre, 'caught' on film. Or Mr Sartre's grave with the collapsed mourner.

Cats on the roof. A man mending a tile or, no, erecting an aerial. Coloured electrical wiring, green, red, black, hangs from the end of a metal tube over the guttering. He steps back onto his ladder; from this distance see the weight transfer from hand to foot over the edge of the tiles. A flat blue sky prepares for Spring.

I have rejected the poet who lisps in numbers. Wry social observation buddy, but dull. Or should I say 'mate'? Invoking the AIF. But I'm not on the way to an order of merit, like Posthume, my friend.

The new bar lights up across the intersection as I fetch pies from last year's version. I read the great narrative poet again after a lapse of years. Looking for a particular passage. And keep going. The trucks have lumbered away. Slip through the cracks of Mondrian's 'Broadway Boogie-Woogie.' A severe Dutchman in love with the future.

18

The day elapses. Aircraft vanish along their great nets. Godfrey Miller. The Pacific. Spelling sheep, these ombudsmen, this diary. Who's letting go of the breath, arguing for the body? Tenuous, like art.

Drinking in the bar metres from the house of the dead man, my former employer. Peak hour, the traffic idling on Elgin. Another boarding house fire. The princess's nuisance phone calls. Opposite, a window, braced with a wood diagonal. Students going home. The collected poems of the San Francisco poet: survivor of Castro Street. Cigar smoke. Tabloid television, when light is loveliest. 'The white knight arrived in a yellow truck . . . Propped up on cushions a fourteen year old leads police in a high-speed chase.'

Cool draft from a swung door. This must be one of the few bars where you can look out into the street rather than be looked at. Red lights winking. The beauty of middle-age: nothing needs proving. They say. A cerulean diagonal between clouds. Artificial green of the roundabout.

I'll resist it all for trivia. Children crossing; the black silhouettes. 'Take the cursor along and touch a rock and fall off.' A man with sunglasses and an umbrella takes the corner. Buckled arrow over Route 34. Acrid cigar smoke – no, it's a pipe. Honey and ash. Luminous petrol pumps. The lit cars, ready for Spring.

Five

2000-2006

Louvres

I opened the door in my face
                                    – Pete Brown

The sky, October,
                    and rain at last
laying the dust of a building site
down the road.
                    Echolalia, the split
of tongues, sublunary things
worry me,
                    a man without socks
'walking',
                    as Richard Thompson,

'through a wasted land'

You love it and have to destroy it. Palimpsest: each a shadow of the one before, the bottles, the tins, the rubber thongs washed ashore from the French island. A faith in things restored, each given their place on the shelves, visible from a dusty couch. You light the torch and hand it on as rain washes grit away from the suburbs

---

The constant rearrangement of furniture
relativities, what lives with you
and what you do without sinks back
under the reshaping atmospheres the albums
uncaptioned daring a narrative
where you start   from there a constant shift
a random play function, boxes of china
sent off to the charity store
things no one wants   the calm

late afternoon light   teetering vee
of a pigeon caught on an updraft

Red November. Poincianas fan low
over the water, sheets of rain
from the northeast blow upward
through louvres. In the courtyard
a pond's surface fractures, yellow flowers
drop from trees   three pigeons roost
on a deck umbrella as the sky veers dark.
A collect of nominals: this, this,
this, with which there can be no argument.

The art of mixing ochre, a series of patient filters   **Bea Maddock**
then the map, a shoreline limned
pale close features, darker distance,
often only a thin line, veneer of settlement
typed names in small print, voices
hung in the air. A lump in the text
whitens, a gouge forms a reservoir
on this periphery done from radials
assuming a centre. These estimated heights
serve to return land once taken;
lend a new register where walls of a gallery
can turn a whole State inside out
as we perambulate across its empty core.

Where do they go, these people
with shopping baskets and scratch tickets
perambulating under the canopy in light rain
the door of the dress shop opened, a mat
placed on the paving and a trolley
hung with price reductions wheeled

to the entrance. Letters circulate,
wires and birds pass through the thin air
darkening above the awnings. What hope
is there for these people.

Boredom as self-recognition (Schopenhauer). As a kind of authenticity
in an age of appropriation. When déjà vu incorporates déjà vu. You have
to name those boats on the river; find words to describe the pattern of
water surfaces, the variation of clouds, shoppers moving according to plan
down the Mall. On a tape I can hear my own voice, aged five, reciting
segments from a school play. But I am now a different organism: not 'the
author' of those books, a cursor moving slowly down a page.

Painted-over windows. What history there
amid the dust from a site up the road;
the solid structure of early twentieth-century
factories, their sawtooths and rusted ventilators,
the very idea of purpose building
anachronistic? Attach here
a history of nostalgia. As though even the air
could be replicated, that history is not
more than we can be aware of now
afloat on this current, a brahmin kite
viewing the before and after of the river.

Along the hallway a face, walking,
illuminated by the glow of a portable computer.
It is a world of epiphany
but where do we take it? Those odd flickerings
at the edge of perception, former inhabitants
from some other completely different set of
circumstances, yes, but also imaginations,
dimensions   patterns of light, sequences

of ones and zeros, a different world
from that in which, as the light in the room fades,
we are introduced to the aether
by the sound of a marimba.

I had been silent for six years unaware that to be the same is to be differ-
ent. I wanted to read unwritten work, absorb influences which did not
yet exist. Returning to former sources six years later they are those works,
those influences.

Cockatoo and wheel screech converge.
An empty chair faces the empyrean
out over the balcony, the rumble of a street:
realism. The damp paddocks
over the river, long mast of a TV aerial
corrosions and unaccountable objects
across a curved roof. The distant suburb
lights up slowly, its main street
climbs a ridge, long dark shape of a primary school
its memory-layer of brick, chalked images
and basketball nets hung over asphalt.

White shapes on a wooden pier
resolve into children   they could
have been pelicans for one moment.
Voices from a garden hard to locate
diffract over a short space   from a bench
where everything dissolves into the present.
Up on the hill over Hamilton, flags
on a mock manor preside over light
which falls on the flood plain around Bulimba.

Philosophy and poetry, runs the weekend news item, are products of long walks (where it can be possible to have them). Is it the movement or the vista? That intently observed, however small and fragile, or the sweep which may be for the historians. A hand-held camera juggled, now pointing at the sky, now the sturdy pair of boots. And it ends up being read by the grammar that holds it together, the sense of a sentence which may be for life. Writing: the product of sentenced beings, knowing and known. As the moon in the water.

What place poetry in a world of commodities? Is it possible to make a 'serious portrait of my times' when the objects I describe will not remain as collateral. Only the geology of this river basin, the paths of its inhabitants obscured by the vagaries of 'lifestyle'. That flood of 1974 released mangroves onto new silt. It's remembered by posts registering the high water mark. Richard Tipping's half-submerged FLOOD at the performing arts museum. But even the houses now mock sturdily their progenitors: 'colonials' with insulated walls. Should poetry feign continuities like these buildings do?

Why should I, who have lived in this country all my life, suddenly feel myself an exile in a distant province? All day and all night the wires and the air itself are galvanized. Information presses upon us. Capital is all mimicry, but with no original; all quotation without source. So these texts might echo those of a distant youth, or those of some complete other out beyond the coulisses of trees and architectures, of ideas floating above the river.

Meat ants trail across a rotten bench plank,
red circle under the plane of a poinciana
the veldt on a river bend. Mississippi steamboat
turning upstream a 'schoolies' disco
(post-examinations) seems top heavy
– the DJ deck. Downriver a brass band

plays something in the vicinity of Dowland
from the park rotunda, heard as far
back as the limbless soldiers' bowling green.

A rusted metal door with porthole   **Leah King-Smith**
down about water level, below the concrete piers
a set of steps to the wet rocks, silt,
probes of mangrove. Up one level
dismantled relics of a turbine, streaked
walls and lines of pipe, large circular openings.
Over this a layering, seated figure
with hands clasped above the head, green
fernlike growths over wall stains and reinforced
piers, the figure in the central of three bays
- that history could be a succession of discolourings
and erasures, of rust and biological cultures
through which the invisible might of a sudden
heighten, apt condensation risen
from a bath of chemicals.

The bedroom ceiling, a distant parallelogram,
sprinkler system as two stars, milky
at dawn from a concealed skylight.

The corner lamp V-shaped like a cocktail glass

water-trickle down internal piping
in the otherwise silence

                              lights on the opposite hill
momentarily black out then resurge, except
there seem fewer orange now than white.

Click of a frog, some pond at the back
of the neighbour nursery. A glimmer,

hand-held light, tent-shaped
near the river bank

                        the tracking blink
of aircraft at altitude heading south.

Shipwreck: **Jennifer Marshall**
                black woodcut shapes
on aniline, engulfed by colour
spread over the grooves,
                                surface textures
the material itself,
                        fine Japanese paper
hung as a scroll a little over a metre

down the walls of a hidden gallery
in the suburbs of a provincial city

where walking under water remains a possibility.

A cable breaks and communication is cut off, or hangs, at least, from gan-
glia partially severed. The line back to poetry a possibility still, but remote
once the disguises are removed. Still, the rattle, the hint of those sounds
and the world they portend. Trying to locate a source somewhere inside
the pipes of a large church organ: that blast of air, of constant traffic. And
the impossibility of grasping direction.

Red halo over Balmoral, strangely inept
title of a hill-suburb, its lack of distinction
save a minimal altitude; enough

for a view of the not so distant city
beyond New Farm, once market gardens and
shipping terminals; Kangaroo Point, sand and mud
till the Story Bridge tied it to Fortitude Valley.
Apartments and plazas follow the river,
appear as though generated overnight. History
beyond the geological is hard to place
in this vicinity, is felt only at night,
the black river its asteroid belt.

Telephone booth lit up in the surrounding dark on an angle below as in
Stewart MacFarlane's painting; it's empty, but seen as a film shot, hints
at the 1940s.

The surface of a river is only one surface   **Lin Onus**
daylight inverts the trees
the fish are inscribed with maps.
The reflections of blue could be realism
but it's realism void of referent: it's style,
another layer another assortment of lights
reached through to touch something which isn't there.
The fish memorialise a place we can only glimpse
as though our world were formed of postcards.
They hang somewhere outside all of this.

Weeks of rain have laid the dust
on the building sites down the road,
girders and cement blocks shaped day-by-day
as unremarkable apartments   footpaths
lead nowhere in particular. On the corner
a lawn has recently materialised
and around into Merthyr Rd sharp whistles
from a poinciana tree locate a dangling oriole
far to the south of its usual course.

Marks on paper, gradations on screen
as ephemeral as the factory light oscillating
upside down in the river: it's there every night
cut by the wake of ferries, resuming
its shape, though this itself is illusion,
there is no permanent, stable form for this
trick of sight. As words hedge
after intent or slant each time they're placed
– even in print meaning shifts,
we are caught by different angles every time.

'It is difficult now to speak of poetry.' My silent habitation, paintings, furniture and books; the dialogue between, my own. This word-hoard otherwise lacks a centre, is flotsam on no certain tide.

The past is not such a repository of dread. The forgotten may be benign and the fears of one generation lapse to curiosity for the next. Once the pieces are assembled everything is understood. A cryptogram may be the clearest means to an end. The house of violence stilled becomes a monochrome world. The image that tracks you may not turn to a set of rails down which you must hurtle. The horizon opens up, smoke in the distance is no premonition nor forgetfulness an unmovable stain.

The island goes Tuscan, forest dug up
to build a nature reserve, the bridge
two lanes to rattle across on the way
to your history, a family's dark secrets
which turn out benign two generations later.
My grandfather, a violent man who made my uncle
line up all the pebbles in the driveway;
threw him out of the house aged nine
with two shillings; then went mad

and died in an asylum, the result of
'insulin therapy' - but that was in 1938. Funny
the past should hover over these clear channels
this drive through brightness, an hour
out of town.

How much of it is the by-product
of parents' fears, incursions from a world
hard now to comprehend, a different set
of rules from those that now toss us.
Even the minutiae are different, atmospheres
like those of movies; a gentle wind
across the river may be as insidious. You throw
your words together, but you are aware
of transiencies and unable to use
tricks of the populists. Just leave these pieces out
to dry in the air: the rattling flags
that will no longer hurt you.

Heavy peppercorn scent in late
November heat outside the Gallery
– redolence – a breeze
up the river, the city in its haze
across Victoria Bridge, the Town Hall
showing the work of an artist
imprisoned in mythology.

Mind has a shape. But the shape of the mind is not determined by mythical templates. The surrealists escaped from the detention centre of naturalism into the high-security prison of mythography.

Air circulates through the latticed wharf
as the brown river laps and bubbles underneath.
A small goanna crosses the path
lifting itself from the hot surface.
Mangroves drag against the current, out
from the tidal rocks.

An improbable group of young demonstrators at the Literary Festival want to get rid of poetry. They complain about having to read anything that is old, that poetry itself is perverse, gives people strange ideas and ruins their career prospects. I too once wanted poetry banned from schools, but for the sake of the art itself rather than the uncorrupted genius of the individual. I'm touched though, by their belief: that poetry could be dangerous.

I don't know what Stephen Spender was thinking of when he compared the pylons to 'nude giant girls with no secrets'. There are two of them here, at Newstead and Bulimba, lines sagging across the river between. At Bulimba they remain visible for a while on tall concrete poles over the rise to the army barracks. At Newstead they go to ground in one of those inauspicious brick sheds, a weed overgrown stretch of land backing up to an old gasometer. These relics of industry will soon disappear (or live on, ghosted, a twenty-first century memory garden neatly planted amid medium-rise and shopping malls).

The apartment, shaped
as a euphonium
into the wrong end of which
butcher birds sing
at 5 a.m.
the inescapable light
descends as
an apotheosis.

Dürer's 'Melancholia', the sharpness of its geometries. A lion asleep amid regular solids: 'golf balls of insomnia'? The weather overhead shifts and changes; its light alters the reality of all things. Against which shapes persist, obsessive and valedictory. Who is the mortal being observing all this? And what are all those shafts of peripheral light?

A pure inscription
of light, moving downriver
erases itself, no time
for the handle of names, dates,
the registration of what passes for fact

From water so foul
fish still can jump
a shore of disintegrating ply
a palm tree, washed
to these rocks from somewhere.
The glare, through skylights
from the windows of warehouses

Charles Olson spoke of a nation of nothing but poetry. But why stop at the boundary? Because poetry exists outside the boundary, it is the peripheral. Poetry is the original cultural study absorbing all the data a grand sweep obscures. A dust of pollen on the page alters the speed of writing. Is this what Olson meant by breath? Book title: poetry and asthma.

The embodiment of knowledge. Words on trade routes, in collision. Chasing the phenomenon of evening light, pollen released from the page. Figures along the banks of the river, an old gas tower, rowing clubs, gaps in the mangrove. The idea of a city, rising beyond the concrete plant, its broken wharves. Weather signals lit up already over the MLC building.

Sunsets and electrical storms
pass over the water
en route to a new continent.
Water itself: iridescent layers
not one stable reality but
reflection on reflection,
depth on depth,
a myth of surface – the painting
one of many spaces before which
figures shift, shading, complicating,
moving on. This part of the planet
is cities, storms, roofs aloft in turbulence.
A map is only one layer of it.

Mostyn Bramley-Moore

Light through melaleuca, no shadow.
Old books, the certainties decades past

up the street which reminds of a country town:
closed shopfronts, verandah posts,

incessant heat; a sense of precariousness.
Its business world, flimsy, could collapse

as figs root up pavement, clothes disintegrate.
The body moves through this, tilts

into the shimmering atmosphere.

Blue Hills 48

Deflected light
of a Vida Lahey intensity

– Vida Lahey, who painted interiors
whose wood blinds throw

diagonals of brightness
against the warm dark; space

polarised, intense, tropic,
as though art and heat might

combust, the luminous aftermath
too instant for climate to abrade or dissolve.

Composizione (1914)

Soffici's painting (my colour photocopy
from a 1946 book):
                        the glass and cup
flattened – glass with a thick base,
cup with an edge turned into a spout
– heraldic almost, either side
above a slice of watermelon, red
white, green: an Italian flag
though with black spots, seeds,
on the red. Near its base
the shape of a fig? (left)
and (right) the letters SOF
stencilled, emerging from a shadow
(of the watermelon slice); the slice itself
functioning perhaps as an A
(for Ardengo), its upward point
continued by an indeterminate
grey shape

The Submerged Cathedral

for Gig Ryan

Pain won't last, neither will beauty;
once everything is registered as atmosphere
only change is left: each waving branch
or fall of light upon water, each
scent or sound suggests as it fades
a world diminished against a myth of plenitude.
Tectonic shifts of orchestral sections
modulate tones a later minimalism will
catch or freeze from the end of a lost century;
amber doorways long encased in soot,
underwater gongs rusted, their particles
cast into colourless depth
beyond a continental shelf.

August 7th

Warm light through tall windows,
tin rooves bleached
under a pale sky,
verandah shadows.
It is the day of the Census
in which we get
to make our lives up
as though there were more
than atmosphere in the account.
Coffee, a newspaper
(the death of Christopher Skase
or should that read 'death'
the tycoon cunningly
disguised as a funerary urn).
I read back over
poems written from memory
casting years of a life
in terms of events
and discover I've got
the situations wrong,
I'm out, in fact
two to three years
in one poem, between
recollection and historical event.
Should I alter the detail,
unravel what
false memory has set up?
or would this allow
too much weight to poems
as documents. The sixties
and seventies for my students
are a blur of seemingly
related events and styles
– for me they're periodised
by year (except for this
mistake I've made in my poem)

so should it matter?
(should it matter to see Elvis
as sequinned from birth,
a product of Vegas, not
Tupelo: RCA Elvis,
not Sun Elvis?). This
is where duration
overrides chronological time,
the space it takes
to drink a cup of coffee
versus what goes down on paper
in parallel, but opening out;
language exiting
through lexical doorways,
living its diverse lives,
enveloping, dissolving even
the maker of mistakes,
his view of rooftops
tricks of light
over an inner suburb.
The very unsettledness
distills a great calm
as though after crawling
through ducts, one had
stepped out into
limitless space.

Difference and repetition

for Ian Friend

The sheet darkens
with added ink, lightens
when the contrast eases.
Enlarged, a comma
becomes a bent lake
on a map, diminished
an impurity in the paper.
From a distance a world
of ruled margins and neat
habitations, closer
it's a mess, repeated over
and over, nearly
but not quite a replica,
a simple pattern with variations,
pier of small black crosses
invisible, almost, against
a sea of hyphens.

The inner western dreaming

A downpour al fresco
on Glebe Point Road:
'coffee time' in the words
of the philosopher, a point
at which everything
and nothing come together
– or else we discuss
respective fortunes
(the 'problem relationship' has no
overarching myth: it is so
and so remains until we
dispense with heroics or
there's a change of weather.
Shaking digits are enough to bear
whatever is on our plate.
Neither Greek nor Biblical
we graze and gaze upon the street
or the street's wet reflection,
our lives tangential, afloat
somewhere to the east of its
severe and perfect geometry.

Blue Hills 50

Damp seats sprayed with some cleaning substance,
two men, edgy, slicked with brilliantine
en route to, maybe, Goulburn.

To sleep, perchance to dream
face forward into the Southern Tablelands
fortified on fennochio, eggs and aspirin.

At Mittagong, the police board
to remove an unruly drunk.

The dry hills, snow-covered last season.
A farmhouse kitchen (1870)
soon to be sold

linoleum squares
and light from all directions.

*

And did these feet in ancient time
step from the kitchen to a techno hum
about the fireplace, high-altitude
bush birds, and a hall clock for bottom end.

I fall asleep to the scent of pot pourri.
Distant rattle of a gate
the sound of footsteps on gravel (as in a novelette)
a streetlight over near the church.

Awake to hydrangeas and gathered wood-fire twigs,
an outside temperature of 16 degrees.

A Grecian urn mimicked in wood, repeated
in ceramic on the table:

the fallen figure from a dark sky
of moons and sea creatures

(which turn out on close inspection
to be a palm frond and the neck
of a camel.

Blue Hills 59

all night long

rain, distant

lightning, fires

rumoured

about the city

Tilt

for Peter Black

The feeling of being here, without explanation, miraculous and terrible in a space where all is gratuitous. The grey mist of rain or the grime of windows. The sharp notes of an unidentified bird.

#

An object never before noticed on the horizon seems to advance and recede though it is stable: a highlit part of a familiar building detached from its customary anchorage.

#

The air is hard and cool. The road goes nowhere under the clouds and the high-tension lines.

#

A landscape opens up and closes in. Its benign features – signage – become, in the stilled image, markers of identity, reminders of loss.

#

The concrete soldier with raised bayonet. The head of a lion. The metal sheaths of streetlights. An invisible flagpole. The buttress of a monument.

#

The inhabitants have left the scene. Their washing, strung across the verandah, a plastic bucket: these are the clues.

#

A country mailbox. Faces of children by a road void of traffic. A handstand holds the planet for a moment upside-down. Figures in middle distance move lightly on its surface.

\#

These people. Do they expect us to know them? To know what is inside this briefcase, on the back seat of that car?

\#

A comforting myth: that the world and all things in it are made of gelatin silver. We rise from a chemical bath and are lovingly curated in acid-free surrounds. Or we are found, curled and cracked in a pile of refuse.

\#

What we don't see in the photographs we take: the slip of a genteel aunt, a disembodied hand, the image of ripe tomatoes on a blue cardboard box.

\#

Tattoos, aniline and permanent, on flesh that withers.

\#

The buildings are all in their rightful places. Then blankness. What if all this were an invention?

\#

All things are concepts. But we are trapped in their consequence. The cash register and the typewriter, archaeology that surrounds us. Our smiles already periodised; those tics that represent an era.

\#

There are no interiors, or what we see is already an interior. Blinding light through windows. Television presuming an outside world.

\#

If you turn quickly the scene will change its shape. Laughter from the street. Your own? Memory is displaced by memorabilia.

#

A reflection in plate glass of a pedestrian walking out of shot. She walks from the bank across a car park. Then she disappears into 1987.

#

Words stare you in the face. Crazy paving and 1960s functionalism become the architecture of despair. A language of shapes dismantled like the genetic code.

#

An old calendar on which events are marked. The taper of trousers passing the demolition site. An engine meticulously restored. Hell for leather. Guarded with your life.

#

The sky darkens over a small town. Gorse on the otherwise bare surrounding hills. Power lines intersect above a memorial fountain.

#

There is no room for nostalgia. The paint is not yet dry on this edifice. Dance steps come straight from an instruction manual.

#

A distance, not local, but from somewhere else. A life led in relation to lives presumed elsewhere. A style reflecting an imagined capital. A capital as fantastic as life on another planet.

#

A dog stares backwards into history like Walter Benjamin's angel. The future, ill-lit, waits beyond the dashboard.

#

The destination of the photograph does not include us or our concerns. It moves away at the speed of light. We remain in our own narratives.

#

Or we are held in another narrative. The lights at the crossing remain forever red.

#

Wind blows the photograph away. The weather in the photograph does not blow the photograph away.

#

A smeared window. Steam and rain. The lit shapes of petrol bowsers.

#

There is no horizon. We are shadows in a moving car. Speed is our history. There are fables behind these images that are forgotten.

#

As though, in waking, benign objects become for a moment the ogres of childhood. Walking in a foreign land where only the accents differ; alternate narratives that might be yours.

The vocation of doubt

(birds on the roof)

(a broken cup)

rain beating in from the southeast

(what I thought was a bird turned out to be a lizard)

poems from elsewhere
a log jam in the mail

the distant rumble of a clothes dryer

(a face in the trees or light on a wall when shadows recede and you step
out into a different place)

(steam rises from the mouth of a human who turns into a factory)

the low clouds boom
a movement in the sternum

(hospital light, the space dematerialising above a bed, the haloed visi-
tors)

dirty windows
prime time television

paranoid response

(an umbrella and a sewing machine on an operating table
'somewhere in the Gulf')

'golf!' he said,

'golf!'

Melancholia,

or the light reflected off metal structures on the roof of the laboratory prior to a storm. The whitish sheets over a darkening sky, a series of regular solids, an obsessive repetition of inarticulate demands. Elsewhere there are holidays, banks circulating notes, a surfeit of intention, but here there are only moments, blocks of consciousness arrayed as patterns in fabric.

When the server goes down the sense evaporates. Corridors become walls, the narrative fades. The novelist has unravelled her plan in which moths have eaten holes. We are left as vegetation in a suburb is a memory of wilderness, a crossed wire bringing back thoughts of the past. Rumour itself ordains our history. Those marks on a fence speak as the lines of a book close upon themselves.

The blue distant hills beyond which is conjecture. The unnamed walking the wall, using up their time in the office. Everything nonetheless has a perfect three hundred and sixty degree clarity, is open to scrutiny. The top of the box removed, the silkworms among the leaves. Those white fibres form an elaborate chain in which the small and large circumferences are cemented forever.

The prospect before us . . .

I go downstairs to buy wine
slightly paranoid the guy in the shop
will be thinking 'you again'
(but it's his job: to sell wine,
so why should I worry). I buy
an Australian shiraz and a
sauvignon blanc from New Zealand.
Upstairs, the heater on,
I read two poems Ken sent.
The builders outside have stopped building
(a third floor of concrete laid today)
and the light begins to fade. It's that
Brisbane winter clarity, sharpness
of buildings in Hamilton and Bulimba,
a white yacht moored on the river
under the cypresses (the old
Rheem factory). A crane hovers,
cement blocks as counterweight. What
will the light be like in Yorkshire
where we'll be in three weeks?

*

                          'everything . . .
small in comparison'
                          (Ken's poem
written during the Gulf War,
our life
          'in the interstices'
'almost furtive'.
                          The poem
a letter between two provincial capitals;
it's a month on, two almost
(since the conflict referred to).
The crane swings to the east
depositing wooden pallets,

hooks up its chains for end of work
(it's Saturday morning) and the operator
descends a ladder passing through hatches.

*

This morning, butcher birds sing near
an open window
                              a gust
flaps the construction company banner
draping a side of the crane
'motionless today'.

Remembered from 'The Country hour' years back,
the theme from 'Blue Hills'
and the river heights
            that Greg McManus once described
            as 'karmically soothing',
though I doubt awareness of water-levels
would soothe now.

What are we?
                        Clerks
enumerating failure?

                        A day so perfect,

wake of a ferry on the mud-coloured river.

September Song

for Ken Bolton & Pam Brown

Bill Doggett and Earl Bostic: Trading Licks
                                    a great compilation
        always reminds me of Ken
                            probably still at work
            in Adelaide, though thinking by now
                                of coffee and writing
                at Baci's (or the Flash),
    Hindley Street.
                        Here it's hot
                                    unseasonable September
                leaves of brown
                                    come tumbling down

        Friday evening of the poetry fest

                                        I'll stay home
                watch the light dim over Bulimba
                                        cook mushrooms
                        à la Grecque
                                (bougainvillea a mass of crimson
    on the balcony, the door
                        waving in the wind though held
        by an elastic fastener).

                    The versifiers will be hot . . .

        I mean hot, not
                    'hot'
                                (a seven part performance
        of the deadly sins sounds deadly)
                                    but it will be great

to hear what the poets in Sydney (and Melbourne) are doing these days.

Bostic's 'Flamingo':

that great blast, rescues a tune

from 'lightness'

(Coltrane would take this on)

half-a-century old

like me

the 1950s

a now unimaginable world

of bright lights, electricity

coloured drinks

'we don't need alcohol

we just like it'.

Whatever you say, Frank.

Are Pam and Jane

wandering Rome

or escaped to a cool villa elsewhere?

Is Pam writing

a view across Trastevere to the Tiber

positioned at a desk in the apartment

as Ken

sets up in the Baci with coffee, cake,

The Guardian,

me

on my back on the sofa

my preferred writing method

. . . from which I watch aircraft

descend over Hamilton,

my friends in their various places

in the fading twilight

like a line from The Star Spangled Banner

a couch

Kerouac was too patriotic to sit on.

*

I cook dinner to
        Danny Gatton, 88
Elmira Street,
        the moon, yellow
gibbous
        over Morningside,
thinking 50s hits
        a teenager imagining
being there
        (on the moon)
        away
from all this
        the cream-puff face
of George Méliès satellite
        (Satellite of love?)

Danny G an heir to this philosophy
        (he
hanged himself in the garage,

        though his music now
seems benign enough

especially the theme to The Simpsons
        or, heartbreak, a version of
'In my room'.

        *

A day later:
I'm sitting on the floor
        (not lying down)
at the Judith Wright Centre
        – the poetry
and Frank Sinatra
        continue –
        Jill Jones
not liking the heat,
        Michael Farrell

('the man wears shorts')

        reading in tandem with Martin Harrison

                                            'Re-

                 New the Word'

    says the poster.

                                Sitting, I view

           legs of the poets

                                ('Gimme da word…'

  said a cartoon in Pam's early book;

                                the frightened reply

      'I … I've forgotten it.')

                                When Michael reads

a guy with beard and sandals

                walks out.

                *

        Home,

           post-reading

the hottest it's been in this room

                  a moon

                            like the one that hangs over

     fields of Shoreham

                   Samuel Palmer's harvest

        except here

                      suburb, not ripened corn

    or both?

          (suburb and corn)

                  that would be Brisbane

      the 'blessed city'

                     as Gwen Harwood had it

         in wartime

         and me

                          an age

       of consumption

            a river-side

of plasma screens.

Who needs the moon?

*

Coffee at Jamie's Espresso

a minimalist model plane above the refrigerator

wire body

pathetic wooden wing

propeller spun by the fan

(what was the line from EM Forster

highlighted METAPHOR

by some scholar:

'the fan rotated like a wounded bird'

a metaphor for poetry?)

Another coffee

'Hi Bronwyn'

is that sculpture on stage

really fish fucking?

The poet takes notes.

New poetry

a veneer of theory

John Forbes

invoked by the multitudes.

Outside, the heat

'neon in daylight'

(the 24-hour grocery)

inside

FAME

I wanna live forever…

No Joke!

*

James Street Bistro.

Will my coffee arrive? (the waitress busy
chatting up the young 'suits').

It does, but it's the
wrong coffee.

'The Reverend David Sheppard … Freddie Trueman
…I'll remember that forever'

Revelation of the year:
John Howard doesn't like cricket.

'Downtown Huddersfield…'

I want a bistro, not an open-plan office.

*

At Vroom, figuring
what it is I like about
music played in cafés

generic 'acid jazz'

neither 'acid' nor 'jazz'

but ok for coffee

('Ambulance Music'

invokes cool for the texters
and me

I'm part of this theatre
wet ink dries visibly

charades of western life

as, at home, on the wall
the fall of Capa's republican soldier, over

an exploding sand dune

somewhere in W.A.

by Tim Burns

(not the Tasmanian Tim Burns

the formerly Sydney one)

rain on the suburbs

drill vibration

from the building site

*

Max Planck said

'paradigm shift always happens

after the funeral'

apparently.

As I age I look

more and more like a thug

waiting

with Basil Bunting

for that fad

(fiction)

to pass.

(at the writers' festival

the mild boredom of hearing people

discuss their work

– it's what you do –

Hello Ivor!

the clouds mass

promising STORM

like the rain last night

horizontal

as I drove Rosemary to the airport

('airpoet'

                said Richard Tipping.

     Thanks Richard.

At the New Farm Deli:

             Alla Zonza!

                          Already

     it's October

Chinese lightning

People of the north are depressed by jacaranda
                               it reminds them of exams
so what of poinciana?
               grades?

   a gale
              blows in from Florence St

                            The louvre mechanism clicks
                  shutters rattle or blow open

'the sun
         has extinguished the glow worm'
                  (Shelley to Byron, via Pam)

   as hot air
              extinguishes a blow-dryer

                            In Italia: sore teeth

        'on a granite bench
            above Circus Maximus'

       Here: lightning
over the Chinese restaurant

                  (a Van Der Graaf generator
          on the Sunshine Coast)

Blue Hills 65

i.m. J.F.

the Domain's still there
glimpsed through The Toaster
its blue foreground
secure under glass
how else to avoid this
expensive design
than face a wall nine years
like Wang Zhen
or you could paint
endless discs that
question the third dimension
as though all this spectacle
were some trompe l'oeil
you had to step through
to reach the mundane

Thirty pieces

for Angela Gardner

1

a suburb's
bars of light
on water where
once a blank
field a blanket
dark across
the river

2

purple horizon radiance
unnatural light the sweeping
ray of the airport red
wink of a landing plane

3

no need of
presence (anyone's)

4

they pass on, pass
it to you, who
don't know what to do
with it, make
a passable effort

5

the expert
lost in a moment
expertise, or lost
in a moment of expertise

6

the turtle beneath the elephant
stands on what?

7

newspapers turn history to pun

why concentrate at all
in this blue haze

8

the problem of agency

9

technology – not, finally, interesting,
its promotion in art a gambit

10

minimalism (not formalism)
– lighter
and deeper

11

temporary space

12

blue hills towards tambourine
the sign

and the seen

13

a col-
umn of
light the
river
warps
as wake

14

the density of air presses in, even in early April as though the black were
pigment massed about the skin. The orange lights with not quite the
clarity of the coming season

15

the knuckles white
of words bracing
about their task

16

to
and
fro
and
up
and
down

walking in Brisbane

17

a cross river ferry
intersects with an
upriver vessel
navigation lights
vanish behind
buildings

a world less rich
under these clouds

provisioned
from elsewhere

18

routines
stitched
together

energies
heavy
in air

19

a mass of tangled rope
a blocked out world of currents

20

the lamplight
of documents
your attention
stolen from coffee

21

the body as
endless surface

a figure eight

22

warm touch
(cold fingers)

integers

23

to
night

and to
morrow

24

the age of the end
of everything

25

incongruous
as a
gondola

26

animal noises
from the court

unseen fireworks
for what?

27

to take it to the edge of sense and then gently deposit it on the bed of
the mundane

28

the tape he sees
recording his voice
age six, gets
littler and littler

the voice heard now
says as much
before the click of spools

29

rain
avails

30

circumstance

a paper cup
in the river

The Nathan Papers 1

eucalyptus after rain, even this, trunks straight or sinuous, reminds of Sydney Long. art has made this environment, its pathways, marked, curve toward the dormitories

*

red mahogany (not 'real' mahogany, just a variety of eucalypt). and in the low-lying areas stringybark and needlebark. the path goes up the ridge. underbrush. a side track revegetating

*

forest on a hill
small brush turkey with undeveloped tail
furiously running

the science of this?   mound building?

*

I never *wanted* to be a poet. not like some people want to be one now. it just happened. and then it was too late to do otherwise

*

the template is buried (or burned), the elsewhere to this *this* for which I function (among others) as an *as if.* 'imagine that all these things you've been taught are meaningless'. or slide into pure consumerism

*

iridescent bird shapes to scare birds off.
bolted shadecloth. fresh wind from the south

*

what if it were all like *déjeuner sur l'herbe*, those figures middle distance of cardboard, people passing in and out of substantiality?

*

my hands are foxed

*

we hear so many accents (at the Capital they hear only their own). in consequence, we are never sure of the sound of poems from elsewhere. this translates into an instability of our own soundings. if the sound of what we read as poetry bears not much relation to the original intent we may be less aware of poetry's musical dimension

*

on the edge of sleep. black spiral binding, blue check bedspread

*

the great cake sails down the river

*

how approximate is this art?

*

an orange flies through the air en route to the dorms

*

'you need a mess of help to stand alone'

*

rain in the atmosphere. the dampness of paper

*

driving to the Gold coast, the theme from 'Get Carter',

and back in the rain Mitch Mitchell's cymbals hiss
on a barely visible road

*

poetry – the opposite of political speech? (that makes you think you *can* understand it)

*

crimson on the balcony against a yellow wash. a thunderous sky dims to bronze and cobalt, then pink and grey, then monochrome

the lit ferries and streetlights

David Roback's effects pedal forces sustain into overtone

*

psychedelic verities

*

the rail track of mild techno. a music that says we are busy, we have things to do

*

small scented bushes fringe the cafeteria

*

Sky News: 'alleged yob speaks',
a panda walks on hind legs,
Saddam in underpants, Kylie's breast ok

*

Mike Parr's drawing. his painterly aspects

Ian Burn's 'value-added' landscapes.

*

no matter how smart you are you can still be floored by Taj Mahal (with the Rising Sons) singing '2.10 Train'

The Nathan Papers 3

a question mark inside a pair of inverted commas

*

4pm parrots
raucous in gutterings
the sky over dark buildings
driving, visor down
to the city

*

the idea of singing a landscape. relate this to the old projectivist talk of
'breathing'. but here the unit has more to do with what is 'expressed' than
with lung capacity

*

container vessel

*

brown needles of sheoak.
a brush turkey, perilous on upper branches

*

if it were a kind of dance, a kind of comedic ballet, it would mean know-
ing where parts of the body might land, on what rock or promontory,
and to which horizon the gestures are made

*

a minute red insect crosses the table between wood flecks and is blown away

*

it's hard for me to conceive how these trees were viewed as 'drab'. subtle rather. how would I manage otherwise?

rain through shadow tents. the girth of those birds. grasping claws, a slippery pavement devoid of sustenance

grey maintenance building through the trees

. . . in which nothing happens

*

anthropologist among the carriers of prospecti, the futures of institution. the wash-up of examinations. unwatched daytime TV. imagine the camera, the casing &c, the blue downlights, fans no longer circulating. a row of bottles, one large one in a wooden case. doors that slide to screen a room. a room in a room

*

eaves dripping in grey light, wet tables out on the concrete.

a bird, smaller than a magpie, darkish long beak, black head, white breast, fawn (or grey) back and wings, a prominent gurgling call

Blue Hills 73

a slight variation
from scrub to open forest

latitude or altitude,
one watercourse to another

whether those verges are
sheoak or eucalypt

– this goes on
for a thousand kilometres

Dogs 3

MORNING

your body remembers its history

*

so close to insubstantial
it will keep

*

'THIS COUNTRY IS MY MIND'

just two minutes after
Les Murray became a republic
somebody cancelled my visa

*

A NATION OF SMALL INVESTORS

we can hardly wait for management
to 'have to let us go'

*

WAR POEM

emotion recollected
in tanks

*

Corrected Poems #1

I have measured out my wife with coffee spoons

*

Market research

'is your poetry poetry like poetry
people who like poetry like?'

*

no ideas but in bombs

*

A near perfect definition of poetry supplied by a Queensland Police traffic officer describing with a double negative a major cause of the Christmas road toll

'momentary lapses of inattention'

*

Life on Mars

'Am I a light bulb?'
                        – tortured Iraqi

No, my friend, you're an
'electric pear'

One-Way Ticket

for Rosemary Hunter

what I have written
I have lost

what's recorded
so much paper and celluloid

the 1974 of desire moves
through its lack of movement

a moment
a memento

amen
a memory stick

a stack
of disks

a pile
of maps

*

worn down by detergents
I'm cleaner and smaller every day

*

the rain it raineth
on a dull tin roof

the anthologies arrive
the wars continue

mere anarchy
etcetera

3 a.m. (or 3 p.m.)
the worst times

death &
taxes

photocopies of everything

*

What I thought was Mo
was Osama Bin Laden
(the face on a half-tone poster)

so where is Stiffy?
(and who is *a friend of the groom*?)

*

spin & spam
vs. art, dust motes

that lightness, something
almost not there

those undeniable venetians
that would argue a pattern

a flying-fish
glued to the refrigerator

a space under the stairs
where memory sits

*

circular paths
a wrought-iron gate . . .

distant apartments
pipes, wind-vanes
funnels

walking figures
backwash
along the rocks

old military medals
account books
chess pieces
a tripod

electrical wiring

a stop watch
a slide-rule
mathematical tables

a microscope

calling cards

a red coat
on a green chair

the smell of fish
fresh marinaded

*

cut & paste:
a generation thing?
mine?   the beginnings
of insincerity?   embrace
of the artificial?

*

there's little sound
from down below

a mattock perhaps
at the edge of the pool

a moment to do nothing

bow wave of the ferry
slight aircraft noise

a chair is not a chair . . .

beached timber

smoke over Mt Gravatt

the tilers insert metal pegs
in the bottom of a wall

hammers echo across the river

already a heat haze at 8 a.m.

*

waves on the ceiling

tidal movements

*

an image of tired people in an airport lounge
painted by Michael Andrews:
The Last of Australia

coffee $3.25
black & white lines
dark wood

in the 33rd year &c (58th)
the body
within its limits

or without

*

be grateful for stairwells

for art at altitude

(a Martin Sharp playing card
circa 1980
in thanks for *East*,

a *tapa* print,

collapsing Cuban
tobacco barns

on a green slope

*

after the encomiums
a bouquet

an apartment of flowers

a fluttering screen

papers in bulk
letters I may never read again

a month before jacaranda season

*

points of light

shadows

gusts

a
lifting
floor

a
door

an orn-
ament

*

over the fold of the map

driving on the wrong side of the world

Six

from
Crab & Winkle, 2006-2008

from September

stillness, at 6 pm,
as though readying a season

I sit in the Gulbenkian
(the nearest boozer)

the numeral 19 amid
the verdure

        (large spaces,
plinths with hewn objects
mimicked by insignias on bins,
neat trees

        the 1960s
thought this the closest
architecture came to paradise

no gargoyles to mock aspiration

HIGH VOLTAGE
          a man
struck by lightning (*timor mortis
conturbat me*) on the side
of a generator

the air thick with smoke

§

rumori, thunder clouds over the campus
(these move rapidly north-east)

a sense of rain

lighten up
(or tighten up –
Archie Bell & the Drells (or
loosen up –
The Nazz –
or the Alan Bown Set (a
different 'loosen up'

                    (O'Hara understood
the importance of all this: a version
of flaneurie
              with a misplaced accent
(mine? here?)
           (*Get the picture?*
Yes, we see.

§

everything at ground level seems quite still

the language of trucks
en route from the tunnel

and news from Australia: the image
of Sasha, Denis and others
in pyjamas, reading books

timor mortis . . .

Sasha's enthusiasms
(how could he *write*, an act
of solitude?)
              Harry Hooton,
a bad poet, but one he cared about
– enough to see the work in print again

O'Hara would have written him up
had he had an O'Hara
                   I remember him

disrobing to white underpants
(a piece on Percy Grainger),

later, walking, with aid
of a stick

§

The couple on the London train – brought together by an introduction
agency? Comfortably middle-class, nervously drinking beer on their way
to a blues concert. They seemed patently ill-matched though unaware
of this, filling each other in with their histories. He was obviously on
the make and lacked a degree of self-awareness. She was quite possibly
alcoholic, not wishing for sexual intimacy but not wanting to be alone.

from October

greyness, and why
a handful of leaves
alone should have coloured

a backward text
erupts through this one

maps show the way to markets
a scale you could step into

where to obtain these portions
these well-lit cover photographs

as Hardy's soil throws darkness
back at the sky

a notice-board pieces our life together
as debt and adventure

the windows (begrimed casements)
impossible to clean

and now, a light from the street
visible through shifting foliage
an almost-silence, mid-weekend
(the denizens elsewhere)

illness is a kind of boredom
– like *money is a kind of poetry*

        intelligible?
        illegible?

        the king's reall or his
        stamped face?

outlines of squirrels in the branches
like 1930s woodcuts by Eric Ravilious

§

these glum bedsits
bred psychedelia

   though the English
in their songs were always
home for tea

(blotting paper with chips?)
    or
mother . . . I'm in a field
somewhere in England
and I've lost part of my brain
     (Jarvis Cocker)

children's books were the oddest things
to fall back on
   a hatch
in the back of a wardrobe
    (a way out
of the Home Counties

from November

remember those who cared about poetry
(as the light dims inadvertently in the bar):
Shelton Lea, once 'dangerous'
in a blue suit; latterly
walking with a stick, a *dandy in the underworld*
whose love for the craft was undiminished
– what place for Shelton in *this* world?
the romantics were fucked, but try telling *him*.
he could have stepped back and conversed
with Dr Johnson, this lost heir
to confectionery fortunes.
                              Alan Wearne
had a nose for the real ones
who'd fit in no survey,
even ∏O, public service anarchist
who wrote better than anyone: a Greek
taking notes from a Turk (Nazim Hikmet)

interrupting my reverie, French lovers on the sofa adjoining, hum of the
bar

what of the pace of art, in a place
where darkness takes over the season?
(sudden applause from the 'drinks' end of the bar)
did the artists 'struggle' for light (more applause),
'chasing' it, for example
in St Ives?

§

logics appear when *the world is*
everything that is the case

all these notebooks, these unanticipated
corners, a map
blown-up, fresh detail inserted

the removal of that rail line
– the Crab and Winkle Way – a path
over the hill to Whitstable . . .

the grand projects become miscellanies

my greatest skill: the ability to 'waste time'

§

we escape our own history
to live in someone else's,
navigating National Trust classifications
(that specify the exact green
of a garage door)

> a stoat
> on the gravel path
> possibly a weasel,
> then, last night
> a small black mouse in the flat
> (maybe a shrew?) hid
> under the bed

from January

on old maps, shifting nomenclatures and variant spellings
(the ghosting too of civic ambition:
streets gridded out in 1920 for a suburb
(of Whitstable) that never eventuated, the space
still rural on the current projection

how, over years
the names shift
a wood relocates
to the opposite side
of a village
a suburb suddenly
disappears then returns
in another place
even then, a title
confidently inked
proves a mistake
there was never
such a place, it
was hearsay

§

a surface of moss,
miniature landscape of another planet,
its ridges and troughs in the slanting light
(in winter you always seem to be driving into the sun
when there is any)

I'm at the window in my Whistler's Mother position

A yellow band above the horizon against which the shapes of trees, bare
branches and pointed conifers, appear as the background of a renaissance
painting (or perhaps the fore-to-middle ground of a Paul Nash). But is it
the case that everything here is like something else? Is this why standard
English poetry is so fond of the simile?

§

June 1958: *The Hotel Wentley Poems*
received in today's post
from Lee Harwood. Who wouldn't want
to have written these? In 1958,
year of the Little Chef,
so why am I &c.
                                  Buy underwear, socks,
Pan Am (the building) *is a colossal*
collection of minimums, so
Ada Louise Huxtable, *New York Times*, 1965
(relayed by Sebastian). But I am not American,
my poems contain no wild beestes, no
lady of the lake, I am
down the road (apiece) from the theatre
where crowds queued in 1963
for Cliff Richard's *Summer Holiday.*

from February

Interlude: Marrakech

my glasses taken away to be
mysteriously mended (orientalism?)
I can't see what I write
(so how do I know what I say . . .?)

a strange bird above the canopy of the *riad*.
what's it like out there
in the lanes we traversed last night
and how will we find our way back here?

                                       with difficulty,
from the square, 'Assembly of the Dead',
adjacent to the *Jardin Foucault*

§

        as those rugs
        this journal
        woven or knotted

enmeshed in the processes of capital,
services (like products) invented;
in the *souk*: more things you don't want
than you could imagine
                          motorcycles
like a fantasy of friends turning up
on two wheels in a French movie sometime in the 1960s
magnified a thousand-fold

the museum must be somewhere
but – don't ask

§

in the pink city, beaks clack
(stork nests on the walls of the old palace).

Evening up on the roof with the satellite dishes, the Atlas Mountains beyond. Car horns and *muezzin* feedback (amplified voices for 360 degrees), a light at the top of the Bab Doukkala mosque.

Islam forbade the illustration of humans and animals but not plants – but then plants are the closest living things to writing, and the two often grow inseparable.

cirrus inscriptions across the sky

§

up in the bedroom, while the others,
drunk on fig alcohol, resound from the courtyard

   malade
    I attempt coffee
the limbs ache, and the stomach
can contain no more

Marrakech in the cool of the morning

a small bird flies in and out
of the room

    my soul, probably

intricate ceilings

     or, Johnny Kidd & the Pirates:
achin all over

   lattice

(*let us pray*)

   or, *mashrabbiya*

blue vase-work and
gold orbs

today, the inner world
(not venturing into the *medina*)

§

what is a bargain?
the vertebra of a whale?
the spine of a salesman?

fifty percent off a life of reduced options?

meanwhile, high-school French
                              (all I remember
of an early textbook:
                    Voici d'abord
                    la tête de Claude

of use in surreal emergencies

Today it was hot, or supposed to be, in the *souks*, but a breeze lifted it and
we sat on the roof of *Chez Chagrouni* in amber light, haze surrounding
the city we will return from, with
 a little joie de vivre
(*not* contraband)
                    which will, at a pinch,
fit a suitcase

from March

By Hollowshore and the Ham Marshes, against a stiff wind along the muddy top of a dyke. Down Oare Creek and up Faversham Creek, the skeletal spire never out of sight. Off the dyke, at low tide, crescent bogs, startled waders, the stiles ('lovers' gates') always a mud patch. Closer to Faversham, the shipyards, then diversion around new housing to Front Brents.

§

People who don't write think of writing as some wonderful emanation, something the author has to get down. Images in film of the writer urgently scribbling. But what if the writing is like *this*, a writing that *pushes* itself along? What if the writer has to force him/her self to write? This is writing as 'work', something the writer may not actually want to be doing. It becomes enjoyable at the editorial stage when all these dull slugs of prose seem to 'light up', escaping their humdrum origins. This is the point at which the writing becomes something *other* than the travail of the writer. It is also the point at which writing is abandoned (though with pleasure often) by the one who might otherwise make a claim for it. It then appears (perhaps) perversely under the author's name but the name at this point has become a mere signifier (if you liked _____'s _____, you'll like their _____). Marshall Berman wrote about the artist character's desire to *see his name in lights*, the modern signifier of success. Mostly we see ours on flickering screens.

§

I sense what Tom Raworth must have felt about the apparatus of poetry and the poetry world. Why, once installed in a prestigious position he chose to write things that defied what an ensconced poet might be expected to produce. I am not such a perfectionist.

§

John Seed spoke against punctuation. He's right for his own practice, the idea that one should set things so that they read *so*. But I have to put

223

this in italics. When I began to write I decided at one point to stop using punctuation until I found there was a real reason to use it. Then I reached a point, years later, when I wanted a kind of Enlightenment absence of ambiguity for which punctuation was crucial. Partly this came from reading Robert Browning's 'Sordello' (as recommended by Ezra Pound). Contemporary critics had lambasted Browning for his incomprehensibility but if you observed the punctuation everything, however convoluted, made perfect sense.

On the sound system, Labelle: *voulez vous couchez avec moi, ce soir* (the comma or pause is important, as Andrew Ford noted when scanning my song '(Do the) Modernism' (*and the name of the dance is the* (pause) *Modernism*). He knew this gap was there despite the absence of punctuation.

from April

at Knole, the weight of history,
the rotting canopy of a four-poster

those fearsome kings and clerics
– enough to bury Vita Sackville-West
were she given the chance
                              (how could Knole
be regretted?

                    adjourn
for lunch, Shoreham,
a fold in the North Downs,
the Darent
            – no trace
of Samuel Palmer, *the most excellent*
Mr B.
              a footpath, signed
under ten feet of water

further up the road,
                        Lullingstone,
its mosaics and hot baths out of place
in this landscape

                    then, nowhere,
the approach to Dartford,
chapels lost with infill

it's Easter

day of the exploding coffee-pot

        §

At Winchelsea, the site of a windmill destroyed in the storms of 1987, as the fallen trees of Knole, only a grindstone and some foundation slabs next to a trig point up above the marshes.

> Ford Madox Ford's house,
> in a back street (the town
> strangely without shops; a pub
> that pretends to have lunch reservations)
>
> Rye, choked with traffic,
> a haze across the marsh
>
> Bank Holiday: a motorcyclists' convention
>
> from Rye Harbour, Camber Sands
> dotted with bathers, the nuclear plant
> at Dungeness

§

The response to Matisse's work: that it looked terrible, but then everything around it started to look dull. Then, almost at the moment of acceptance his work was seen as retrograde, the Cubists and Surrealists had seen to that (though Breton had earlier championed him). The paintings done in Nice in the 1920s, products of existential terror viewed as comfortable domesticity.

from May

The 'future' of the Futurists was largely the absence of a past. They recreated the winged victory as a fast car, as if, like the symbolists, speed itself, an idea, meant more than the thing. So – lines of force. Synaesthesia: coloured music, the curve (of beauty?) as well as the diagonal and the triangle.

Then Marinetti, at sixty, enlisting, or trying to; Boccioni killed by accident, not warfare.

The dimmers come on. But we are Futurists in here! We demand light: the assassination of the moon! Death by vapour trail!

I'm not exactly observing my surrounds, but this *is* a theatre, a space, open, for whatever takes are taken.

Harry's avant-garde sensibilities: that one must be open always to performance (this may be Futurism's real legacy, those eruptions of sound, those uncontrollable musics.

The notebook too needs its infusions, its discrete noises. Discredited modernity doesn't mean a retreat to *chaise longue* and chesterfield.

§

minimalism
it's what I do

from June

a hole in a wall
leads into a garden

allotments and duck ponds
sheds and bridges

as close to willow pattern
as the Home Counties allow

light leaving the sky
the sick-bed

immersed in typography

all the books I may/may not read
or write

what would hold English matter
as 'Blue Hills' held Australian?

§

why is there sand on the French coast
and stones on the English?

the same chalk runs beneath

rain damaged frescoes
a slight psychedelic Virgin (Boulogne)
in a boat, waves
of frozen cement

In the square of the 'new' town a market gives way to a political meeting
which in turn gives way to a wedding. Black 1940s Citröen, bonnet up,
waiting.

Mon oncle,
south of this
out of Amiens
an English graveyard
09/08/1918
Aust^n Light Horse
Vignacourt, some miles
W. of Villers-Bretonneaux

out from Calais, glare and mist

does the land appear because you want it to?

false patches of light on the sea
then, dimly, Dover and the Cliffs,
a washed out strip between cloud and water,
outlines of the Castle and docks

a daguerreotype

§

The importance of strange poetry, of unfamiliarity.

a mind always elsewhere
not focussed on text
but allowing it to shift
as a film before perception
odd detail in clefts
part of the net seen clear
the weave otherwise vague

from July

at Dungeness, all is aftermath, dropped on pebbles
as habitation, industry, trash.
to mark any part of this 'private'
is senseless, over it
the nuclear plant (its own planet)
secured on a flood plain

if art can be made of old rope
shoes and driftwood
what follows?

everything here is deposited
everything can be carried off

§

I have become a relentless empiricist. But empiricism carried to an extreme becomes a kind of religion – a theology at least – where everything (the impossible!) must be included. As, on my grandfather's orders, my uncle counted and positioned stones in a driveway.

an empiricist, and a minimalist, for whom
texts strip down to phrases of music
and art is a way of passing time

Remember that critic who suggested that my work was 'the poetry of lists' (I don't think she meant this to be flattering)? There's a philosophy that assumes all things are lists, or made up of them.

little contingencies
for whose delight?

Are the poems charms against death? As though to keep singing (as the birds) denoted existential terror.

§

you grasp a piece of conversation
hang on after the moment has passed
as though it were an object not a process

yet your writing has never done this

from August

the gnats 'wail'
pas de deux
blackbird and thrush

'goose bumps'

beaks scratching the guttering,
manic at dusk

        tomorrow's storm brews
        over the Shipwright,

        over duckboards and clinkers,
        the high-tension lines

        banking toward Whitstable

        the wind will probably
        lift these plastic tables tomorrow

        . . . or tonight

        on a mown lawn, in a ditch
        beneath the dyke

        weather bearing up
        from Sussex

        – will I be wet
        by Faversham Creek? –

        my office
        in various places

where this
gets written

the rumble of an airliner
above these clouds

this country

a toy giraffe
abandoned in the garden

across the marsh
a wind farm, white

under broken cloud

the black sail
of a yawl

a large blue heron
risen from the reed beds

§

stillness and mildness
presaging autumn?

red trellis
over darker brick

scraped timbers

layers, like
A Furnace

a smudged page
submerged

out the window
bright berries

listen to Little Barrie

§

burnt umber on black, shapes dissolved
for which the best light is half-light,
illuminating but not reflective

a painting you can always almost see
– this on the side wall of a long room,
its far end, odd-shaped panes, sunlit,
a parallelogram on the carpet

coloured glass bottles
                              the pattern
subsuming everything, unrolled
as a rug, but endless
                              fading soon enough
as though a season were accomplished in moments

how much of it 'adds up'?

a buzzing insect enters then leaves the room

Seven

2007-2017

Letter to John Forbes

lit up in a window
with a burger & glass
of African *chenin blanc*

I'm reading the later Creeley
on Charing Cross Road

you, ten years back
in limbo (Melbourne)
of which you made the best

I inhabit an England
you mightn't recognise
though you would have read
the fine print that led here

(the market *didn't* decide
in your case).

will I echo Le Douanier, who
celebrated Picasso as 'traditional',
himself as 'modern'?

maybe

this notebook's
no 'art pad',
nor is this place

(everyone behind the counter
is from Poland)

the music:
'I am a cauliflower'
misheard from the Stone Roses

opposite: BUDWEISER,
ENGLISH BREAKFAST
'OPEN',

the only art here
is civic (a 'water feature'
from the seventies)

the buses all head north
to Clapton Pond,
but I'm southbound
for The Cut, Southwark,

poetry, spotlit
on a tiny stage

Grenadines

to arrive at a place
without baggage

to leave with
spectral architecture

a barman
fluent in Scouse

labelled
'the prick from Cadiz'

a river, disappearing
under a town

*

the pomegranate
a toothed apple

as wall relief
or bollard

*

Ortiz
viewed Albaicin
as dice, rolled
down a hillside

*

Images of two monks (Carthusians?), one
pierced by a spear, the other
bullet wound in the chest or
hatchet in skull.

Who are these people?

*

sword and
cross:

the cassock
goes well with

'fruit salad'

*

Baroque is
'shock and awe'

you see the virtues
of Rococo

Written in a Kentish Pub on Hearing of the Death of Jonathan Williams

a
generous man

a modern
epicure

gone from
our midst

(I could knock
together something

like gammon &
mushrooms

(here, the schoolteachers
figure pints will

write reports.
another Bishop's finger?

yes, and
in memoriam.

for J.W.,
what?

photos of
Kent's finest?

(this Thatcherite
province, its

councils
comprised of

Tory
stayputs

the idiots
of small business?

(blue bins
appear

then dis-
appear

the populace
have no-

where to
put them

plastic bags
resume).

what's for
Jonathan here

the gastro-pub?
(fine unless

you contract it
(gastro)

a walk, coast
to coast

drive, for coffee
fuel

('O'NAN's
AUTO SERVICE'?

it's a world
of open

parentheses
a world

minus J.W.
'You can tell

white trash, but
you can't

tell it much
. . .'

(or you could
give it

the Bishop's
finger?

a man
in absurd

green hat
represents

St Patrick's Day
(when is it?)

now, here?
nowhere?

or a joke
(I don't know

as I don't
so many items

of customary
ritual

(no hot-cross-
buns

in this town,
Monday,

the bakery
closed.

tonight, here
in the pup

(the 'pup' . . .
no, the pub

(in the Sun
where I sing

escaping
plumbing

re-
sponsibilities, re-

views, a Yeats
biography

the drummer
from Caravan, again?

(the sadness,
progressive rock

in the provinces
in, on

or about
the premises

incognito no less
(a glow

of light
behind glass

over the bar:
pump

& circumstance,
a trail (trial?)

of spilt beer
(spilt images?)

*lachrimae
rerum*

& death
(over all)

jamon?
gammon?

(on the Ham
Marsh?

J.W.
R.I.P.

Angles 13

At night

all things sleep
save rats

in the walls
(wondering if

they're any good
or not)

outside, yellow
streetlight on gillyflowers

a moss rooftop,
who knows what con-

stellation overhead
or the whereabouts

of ducks at 3 a.m.

An Italian Lake

one side shaded
for months; the other
plentiful olives, a house
on a steep hillside.
this is 'a speechless place'
says the guide: meaning
neither incomparable
nor unspeakable;
'sightless' perhaps:
a wall of shuttered villas
owned by footballers
and movie stars

Dogs 4

MOHAIR

her suit
hirsute

*

GHOST WRITER

advice:
add
vice

*

subtleties
subtitles

*

LANGUAGE POEM

alimony
al limone

*

aphasia . . . that's
the word

*

A Salute to the Cambridge Marxists

If you're not at the High Table
you're not in the room

*

a fine day in
the decline of the west

*

a plaster dog and cat
chained to the shopfront
of the RSPCA

*

after Pete Brown

I stumbled into the john
in the John Curtin
and saw, written
on the tiles 'John
Forbes is fucking awesome'

*

the new avant are touchy
like movie stars

*

Barcode   *for Alan Halsey*

if it's not a free country
at least it's a free house

*

The Ghost of WCW in a Faversham Pub

'I'd love to go back
to Acapulco

it was so different
and so easy'

*

A Jonathan Williams moment in Hay-on-Wye

GIANT BOOK SALE
at Three Cocks

*

After Harvey Shapiro

I read the Hebrew 'bereshit'
as 'bear shit'.
In the beginning was the bear.

*

Universal Toilet

this train has,
says the 'onboard manager',
a 'universal toilet'

*

do horses dream
of hamburgers?

*

ADDRESS

High Dudgeon, Kent

*

at Seven Dials: 'psychic readings –
appointments not always necessary'

*

THE LOUIS JORDAN/WCW MASH UP

there ain't
nobody here

but us
white chickens

*

A SHROPSHIRE LAD

Much Wenlock
about nothing

Allotment #2

At the Norfolk Arms
pressed tin and Corinthian columns
smoked *jamon* and cut glass,

a gilt Madonna hemmed
by dried peppers: W1 *espanol.*

This neighbourhood's Georgian,
the pub, named for Norfolk who?

Thomas Howard, the 4th duke,
Norfolk in Sussex, recusant?

The Spanish barman says
of the wine list I stare at
'the most expensive is the best'

I remember instead the edict
on an album cover
(*The Dictators Go Girl Crazy*):
'quantity *is* quality'

Allotment #4

William IV, Shoreditch

> will anyone be here?

I have books to sell (ha ha)

> and pints to go before I weep

I have at least figured out what to read
(give or take)

> and, is it,
> Apache?

> not the Shadows:

a new version, ornate
with percussion, brass, organ and bells.

> no sign of the poets . . .
> or the audience
> they're all, I suspect
> at Allen Fisher's lecture

the sardines are good, with new potatoes, green beans and capers

> scales fall from my teeth
> if not my eyes

sufficient is the funk unto the day

> still nobody here

though the guest beer
stands me well (if that
be the expression

> in, on, or about
> the promises

premises

strange rhyming voices
and clinked glass, a party
on the opposite table

                                    the one-eyed
                                    spill fewer beers

and the bust of (Beethoven?) blinded in one eye
on the upright,
a candle, stuffed birds,

                                              art,
                              a blurry Rowlandson?

still no poets

                                        the music
                                        ramps up

I'm sonically enabled

                              13 ways
                              to stuff a blackbird

I'll be pissed off
if not pissed

                              a plucked guitar
and a 'sincere' piece of 'spoken word'

                              (Solomon Burke would do this better

'I'm so glad to be here tonight,
so glad to be in your wonderful city . . .'

                              (Everybody needs
                              somebody
                              to love their poems)

In advance of the broken arm
(the Broken Arms Hotel)

                              Simon arrives.

there are now four people
(plus the poets)

                    an audience

Fat Billy on the wall

          (William IV)

Allotment #25

'deep and crisp and even'
the snow

rudbeckias
brought down

finally (I thought)
spring back

with snow melt,
pinks too, as

trucks jacknife
on the motorways

Allotment #28

a dose of 'the finger' (Bishop's)
and the fire

someone else writes in this room, or types
on a notebook
                        a poem
a report (or both)

it's dead quiet on the street
where earlier in the day a Dutch truck
delivered flowers

a man with a black hat and cloak enters
(also with a folder)
                                 so the room has now three (3)
readers, writers, reporters

a season by the fire or
Un Saison d'Enfer

Allotment #34

back at The Sun
                        (beyond the . . .

I graph all this, with flattened accent
(drawn but not glottal)

(the test: 'This is Illyria, lady')

(I myself am a bracket,
a footnote
                        but this is as it should be

the smudge of a glass
set down on paper

this   this   this

Allotment #44

I'm seated at 'my' table in the corner,
a view of the bar. Writing on the window reads:

THE SUN INN

~

FINEST ALES and PORTER

which is almost POETRY

> someone speaks in a Slavonic language:
> the words 'Casablanca' and 'Gestapo' audible

I keep thinking of John Forbes' line:
'spent tracer flecks Bagdhad's night sky'
that I would hear as 'Spencer Tracy'

> this is a Humphrey Bogart occasion

these men, in camouflage,
leave the bar

Allotment #52

Robert Duncan at
           Bernie O'Regan's?
a hand
           measuring beats
                      insisting community

 some eight of us,
           Melbourne, 1975
(my clothes testify)

           occult equals outside the purview
           of the Enlightenment.

                      I'd sourced modernism
for convention
                      grew later
to love the madness of those
excised from history

Allotment #61

my head missed the beam
the back door of Monk's House
but scraped the gutter

I touched (illegally) Henry Green's
Pack My Bags (the books
not to be handled)

they would walk between houses
across the South Downs,

felt the cold less than us
though servants dug their cess pits

from rear of the vegetable patch
the land falls away to the Ouse

where she sank, Mrs Woolf,
weighted by stones

Allotment #71

The front bar of the Bear,
quiet at this hour, a smell of Brasso

and a hint of rain, of more perhaps,
a speckled pigeon crosses the square

passing the headless dummy outside the Op Shop,
Carter's Newsagent closes,

the pitch of the roof above the stationers
almost mansard with lead ridges

everything grey and white (white
of buildings, grey of sky) and red brick

Allotment #72

plants hang from window boxes above the wine merchant
(boarded-up)

the sweeper grins as he shovels trash

tattooed on a man's neck
outside the Lord Russell:
LARRY
14-02-11
HONEY

then 'Telstar', Margaret Thatcher's favourite tune

a herald of free-enterprise?

a hint that the rich might, fifty years on,
escape this ruined planet?

Down Marchmont Street
                                    little flying saucers
glide along a sushi counter
all that is solid melts into air

Allotment #74

long grass, gnats
to shoulder height,

the North Sea:
distant, cerulean, a pink strand

far side of the mud flats,
the racket of migrating birds

Allotment #93

All Hallows approaches
the bar strung with rubber bats,

telescopes, astrolabes
obscure the windows.

Pepys drank in this pub
(the Thames, Wapping

above the tunnel
to Rotherhithe)

further out, rotten wharves,
hulks on the estuary bed

empty sea-forts
subject to slow rust

A short history of France

for Jane Zemiro

In Toulouse winged beasts
line the courtyard of an old convent,

there's a room of Romanesque capitals,
large paintings of wars

fought elsewhere, mountains
closer than they are now.

The last city defences
demolished 1820,

red brick channels
the Garonne's rapids,

trees snagged on rocks
from a recent flood.

Movement of wind through plane leaves
is pointillisme.

In the riverside bar a student reads
One Dimensional Man.

Postcards from Massachusetts

for Jess Mynes & Ruth Lepson

1
dun home counties sky

2
aloft, between Porcupine Bank
and the Charlie Gibbs Fracture Zone

3
under Orion (O'Ryan)
50 miles from Gloucester

traceries in Lincoln's night air
pine needles on the skylight

4
an orientation speaker with irritating voice
traverses Harvard Square, as I arrange poems
on the steps of the church

5
air-conditioning blasts the curtains,
an orange crane swings south,

Bunker Hill viewed at an angle,
the Charles River over there

I keep thinking 'Dirty Water'

6
turn up the heat and order in

7
Concord is 'conquered'
rail trucks overgrown in a siding

Amherst, Ms Dickinson's house,
her grave, back of seventies shops

8
reading at the café-bar in Wendell
I find myself 'leaning on the john door'

9
I feel like the English character in an American movie:
'I've really had a jolly good time thank you'

10
tailback at Concord roundabout

no rest from this condensery

11
everywhere's a building site
this whole part of Boston is money

the coastguard slips out
by the Institute of Contemporary Art

12
PARADISE SELF-STORAGE
near Swampscott, where Eigner
looked out on the street from a glazed porch

then Salem in angled sunlight,
at Gloucester The Cut,
tyre rumble on Blynman Bridge

this republic (and its Republicans)
viewed in gloom
from Half-Moon Beach

13
bagel parlour talk:
'why did they axe *you*?'

14
Halloween's een
a dark blue sky behind apartments
thinned out yellow leaves foreground

and then Paul Kelly in the foyer:
'have you ever seen Sydney from a 727 at night?'

15
Logan: the Durgin-Park Bar
'established before you were born'

candidate Scott Brown's fake tears, and
'now the Panthers have their first
give-away for the night'

16
the torn edges of both continental shelves,
suddenly a horizon,

somewhere down there, a disused shed
in Co. Wexford

17
on Southeast Rail
the voice of England: 'All our toilets
are in working order this morning'

Readers

for Tony Frazer

André Kertész photographed them
hunched over a paper,

seen from above on a rooftop
or below on a fire escape,

shadowed in a park,
or lit up on a bench

knees holding a book,
a cow over this one's shoulder

Differant curioes

for Jann Chambers & Greg Maguire

once you could see the trains from this yard
now it's a forest,

Illawarra flame in the canopy,
magpie lark on the floor

someone sings from the adjoining flats

*

a geography: gullies
empty into Botany Bay via Cook's River, Wolli Creek

the bay now largely clean,
at La Perouse white beaches,

a former snake pit,
a fenced-off church

a laneway in Pyrmont called Cadigal

*

words slide around in their possible configurations
a concatenation of rail trucks parse the sentence
as idle leaves droop

how much weight does a tree invest in dead branches?

Sydney moisture: at once cold and hot
densities of air
                    undergrowth of text

I read the small print of album covers

*

this room in half-light
of paintings 'by various hands'

the objects in Ken Searle's work: louvered window, tiny corner of
red-yellow cloth in another distant opening; foreground: paint peeling
off the edge of a table, red and yellow handle of a kitchen utensil (an
echo)

the brown bottle appears concave

*

spanish moss above wrought iron leaves

a shadow of clothing on the grass

Goodbye Ava Gardner

for Cameron Lowe & Tim Wright

Fly in from the east, the Ninety-Mile,
mud islands off Wilson's Promontory,

                              to this place

of long cool terraces, fanlight
over front door, a gap beneath,

these wide streets, their median strips
broad enough for picnics,

an occasional breeze
from Hobson's Bay

this corner of the city

*

The Age hits the porch

cloud, west beyond the chimneys, masses,
hints a storm

someone practices bass
I read the street directory

white roses, red geraniums,
a backyard otherwise bare

a mess in the street
now gone (Amess Street)
bar the boxes

*

                              'almost all of Melbourne was there'
if not in Italy

at least in Lygon Street,
                         the Università
where the old Italian boss takes our photograph,
pretends to pocket the camera and run
                                      (an old joke
but he does it well)

was that a tram
or the sound of rain approaching?

*

the space of this inner suburb is all sky,
a ridge down to Carlton
                         (from Elgin Street, the dip then, distant,
those childhood mountains
                         the Dandenongs

*

all those years of illegible script
(notebooks from this city date back to sixty-eight)
the scribble dilates,
                      odd moments comprehensible

a blackbird (female) scrounges through bark chips,
part of what looks like a ruined pediment,
a head, maybe, like the robot in Ken's backyard
                              'look on me ye mortals…' &c

all this under the shrub rose, the wrought iron lattice,
the open garage, its shelves of bags containing other bags

peculiar austerities of other people

*

the superimposition of pattern is African:
Japanese fabric under a check picnic rug

on a 1970s sofa; stripes against animal shapes;
a Persian and an Afghan carpet

then I make a milk run to the Vietnamese grocer

*

the pen runs out
(as the toothpaste, the shaving cream)

adjust to leaving here
                                    'the last place on earth'
once a movie with
a bored female lead

we chase the dark
across the map
                        'blizzards in Britain'

diagrammatic dunes west of Muscat,
a miniature sun above the Queensland coast

and hours to go before I sleep

A bridge

steps

pockets of colour

vermilion on the far side

an escalator uphill

Pessoa (bronze)

sits outside the café

Da Silva's splinters of light depict

a city of depth and distance

the wings of a butterfly   *borboletta*

dry underleaf

in a run-down garden

broad harbour beyond the Praça do Comércio

a climate   blown eastward

under the bridge called April 25th

Vedute

Palermo

It could be out of Francesco Guardi
this city, though he was Venetian,

these buildings with grassy pediments,
everything run down

hinting at greatness, then
masking it with concrete.

In the Villa Giulia by the central fountain
the busts have mostly lost their heads.

Cats doze in the Orto Botanico
between potted succulents; the dogs,

stray but docile,
sleep on the footpaths

*

Demolition

A square of houses, windows bricked in.
Around these, dust, gamblers, the edge of a market.

A block away streets resume their regular pattern

*

Items

Mario Sironi's grey street, 1920,
a small truck, blocked
by tram number 304,

a hint of the traffic outside now;
Renato Guttuso's nude, made of
newspaper; these

in the Galleria d'Arte Moderna.
In the Galleria Regionale
Antonello da Messina's Madonna,

the head of Eleanora of Aragon
by Francesco Laurana,
smooth enough for a later century.

Outside in the courtyard
an attendant, snaps off as gifts
cuttings of aromatic plants.

*

BAROQUE

The baroque was always an add-on:
facades tell of uncertain gravity,

painted ceilings,
features 'to pass out under',

the Battle of Lepanto in gold on white plaster,
something to take the breath away

*

CATACOMBS

They grin or howl,
heads twisted from bodies

each hangs forward
unsupported by neck muscle

some in bow ties
some in moth-eaten trousers

those in the professions
have their own aisles

those of the cloth
the darkest spaces

all are covered
by thick dust

*

Contours

After Termini
the train cuts inland

up a river valley
towards a divide;

market gardens
give way to dry country,

eucalypts, referred to
by Lampedusa,

olives
and prickly pear,

uplands, ploughed
within an inch of erosion,

precipitous rocks: signs
of slippage,

boulders, break the flow
in ravines; above,

a village, Sutera,
circumnavigates a peak.

*

Agrigento

The cathedral threatens collapse,
a shoulder of the hill northward

prone to subsidence. The steps before it
fenced off, contain

running shoes filled with concrete.
The ruins are a few miles out,

Africa a little further.

Floriana

beyond the redoubt,
the eighteenth century:

a Mall lined with
hollow busts

(cast iron) of
notables;

beyond this, food
left at the garden gates

eaten by cats that sprawl
as signatures

A room, Venice

a steel beam supports a wood floor,
grained and splintered, nail-holed,
edged with concrete, the remains
of piping;
                           a clockface
holds between stars two fish,
the hands stuck at four forty-two

An Excursion and a Visit

i.m. Lee Harwood

a cellphone photograph
(blurred) of Chanctonbury Ring
up from Buncton chapel, 2007

trees mark the site, partly flattened
by gales twenty years back, resuming a shape,

a semblance of high wind,
clouds massing, the profile of a hilltop.

a mechanical duck pedals a tricycle
across a floor in Hove,

the sea down the road
a limit horizon (described as a wall
                    by Paul Evans

a ruined pier
rusted metal flutings

                    the Regency had time
for such amusements

In Devon

1

Late sun in Shaldon,
inward tide

LADY ALEXANDRIA, SMARAGD, and CALYPSO (Dutch flags)
anchored at evening

red stone, red sand,
lichen on the slates

2

out of puff
on Picket Head Hill

the distant coastline
– west, not south – is Dorset

a bird in the long grass: Chiff Chaff (?)

3

Bronze age and 14th century:
either way, a use of stones
under Dartmoor skies

(its prison a panopticon;
the nature of internment
19th century and Gothic

the nature also of isolation
once 'the mists descended' &c

Ponsworthy such a village
cut off in winter, possibly

at Widecombe, cows
use the main street

4

The Salty breaks up into lagoons, then channels;
a green gap is suddenly filled by a train
for Plymouth or Penzance

the docks empty for the next three days,
two trawlers the biggest vessels in the estuary

5

the 1920s stretched through the next decade
at Coleton Fishacre, home of the D'Oyly Carte
(little sense of depression
in the entertainment industry)

hair tongs, hair dryers,
a flushing sink, down which
to empty piss-pots

an imported garden
– eucalypts, and succulents –
drops steeply
to Pudcombe Cove

6

rain drives in from Dartmoor
clouds move southeast,
crows circle,

a flurry of gulls and diving birds
skim the surface

the drizzle hits
on the ferry from Teignmouth
and holds,
the Salty fading
through a glass balcony

7

there are now three (3) trawlers,
no ships

the inhabitants
tucked up
in their pubs

even the gulls have gone elsewhere

what's the Scottish word
: dreach?

a silhouette of the peninsula
its spires and towers:
religious, civic, navigational
as the first lights come on behind the docks

8

a new visitor
PAPER MOON   (blue – no discernible flag)

9

walk up the estuary
via a kelp shore
(the Templer Way)
in light rain
to a village pub
(The Wild Goose)

10

this morning's clear,
PAPER MOON visibly risen on the water
white sand hangs in the air above

Victorian attics aligned up the hill
view the entrance;
the green slope over Teignmouth
drops sharply, far side, to Babbacombe Bay
as though the whole of life was a cutout

a solitary shoe on the floor

a distressed piece of timber
on which you expect cuneiform
next to the television remote

11

the Channel as an escape route,
a sense there's a world out there
(alien to many)

12

back on the Templer
to St Nicholas, Ringmore,
mudbanks and mussel farms hidden by the tide

a man waters a rusty vehicle
marked AMBULANCE

13

the M5 to Taunton and back

showers

'delays expected'

14

the next day, PAPER MOON's gone,
SMARAGD back from Bordeaux

Mitchell's Fold

for Keith Jebb

From White Grit
a farm road

then moorland,
a broken circle of stones.

Two joggers approach,
navigate the site

as though touch
could transfer energy,

otherwise: silence.
Wales is blue haze,

a kite hangs
above the border

Lightning Source UK Ltd.
Milton Keynes UK
UKOW04f1609100118
315901UK00001B/21/P